Puffer Fish as Pets.

Freshwater Puffer Fish facts, care, information, food, poisoning, aquarium, diseases, all included.

The Must Have Guide for all Puffer Fish owners.

by

Elliott Lang

Published by IMB Publishing 2013

With thanks to my dad for teaching me all about Puffer Fish.

Also thanks to my wife and kids for sticking with me throughout the many hours I spent writing this book.

Table of Contents

Chapter 1. Introduction

When it comes to aquariums, I have hundreds of memories of them as a child. There was something wonderful about watching the fish swim around under the lazy light that parted the waters.

It was peaceful and a little bit magical and I have never seen a child who wasn't delighted by an aquarium. For me, it was probably in those first childhood memories that my love for all things aquatic began.

I loved fish and had several of my own aquariums before I was even out of high school. There was no doubt that, for me, a lifelong passion had begun.

Over the years, I have owned and cared for countless aquariums. I have kept freshwater aquariums and I have branched out into the colourful world of saltwater aquariums.

I have continued to learn about aquariums and have been able to adapt them to suit a multitude of fish species, but one that I have loved for years is the puffer fish.

Whether you are familiar with the puffer fish after seeing them in person or whether their interesting traits have caught your attention through fiction, it is undeniable that the puffer fish is a fish species that is quickly gaining popularity.

In fact, it is a species that are finding their way into the aquariums of many hobbyists and enthusiasts. They have beautiful colouring and are so full of character that they often add a little something extra to a tank.

In addition, these wonderful fish can work in both freshwater and saltwater tanks and there are several sub species that an enthusiast can enjoy.

While there is so much richness in the world of puffer fish, one thing that I have found is that there is no richness in the information about them. Many people, who are just starting out in the world of aquariums, do not have any information on how to properly care for a puffer fish.

This leads to puffer fish not remaining healthy in their habitats and becoming more of a frustration than a joy to keep.

I know, personally, that puffer fish can be an amazing addition to any aquarium and they really don't need a lot of extras in regards to care. Still, there are a few things that you should do to make sure your puffer fish is healthy and stays that way.

That is really what this book is all about. Bringing you the wonder of the puffer fish while giving you all the important information on how to properly care for your puffer fish.

In this book, I go over everything from the best types of habitats, feeding your puffer fish and what to expect from the puffer fish in your tank.

In addition, I will go over breeding your puffer fish and how to determine the sex of your fish. This is a comprehensive guide that will give you all the information you need to have an aquarium that will showcase and sustain your puffer fish.

Chapter 2. The Beautiful Puffer Fish

So, you are interested in owning your very own puffer fish. Well, the first thing that I would like to do is say congratulations. Puffer fish are a very unique type of fish that has the ability to inflate its body to several times, even up to a 100 times, larger than its actual width.

For anyone who is interested in owning a puffer fish, it is this trait that can make them desirable; however, there are many more reasons as to why puffer fish are desirable to everyone.

In this chapter, I will go over a variety of facts about puffer fish and will go over exactly what a puffer fish is.

1. What is a Puffer Fish?

While we all have some idea of what a puffer fish is, it is important to start with this before we begin working on any other section of this book. Puffer fish are fish that can be found in fresh water, salt water and brackish water, which is a combination of fresh and salt water.

They are characterized by their human like faces and their large fleshy lips. They are also characterized by their ability to puff themselves up when they are frightened or feel threatened in any way. Puffer fish can be a range of sizes and colours but they generally have the same appearance, which I will go over in greater detail in the chapter on puffer fish anatomy.

Puffer fish are known by a number of different names including swellfish, balloonfish, blowfish and bubblefish. Their Latin name is Tetradontidae and there are over 120 different species of puffer fish all over the world.

Generally, puffer fish live in temperate climates and are usually found in the tropics.

2. History of the Puffer Fish

Puffer fish and fish relating to the tetraodontids family have a very long history. In fact, puffer fish are believed to have evolved between 80 to 101 million years ago, although it is not clear of the exact dates.

While puffer fish have a long history of evolution, the actual history of it as an aquarium dweller is unknown. What we do know is that puffer fish are commonly used for fugu, which is a sushi made with puffer fish. This dish has been documented as far back as 2300 years ago in Japan and even as early as 400BC in China.

Despite being a delicacy for many Asian countries, puffer fish, with their human like faces and dog like personalities have quickly become a popular choice for aquariums over the last 50 years.

Unfortunately, puffer fish do not breed frequently in captivity so the majority, if not all of the puffer fish that are in aquariums today, have been captured from the wild.

3. General Facts about Puffer Fish

Now that we have gone over what puffer fish actually are and have had a brief look at their history, I feel it is important to go over a few facts about puffer fish.

Do puffer fish make good pets?

If you are looking for a pet that you can take with out you, then no, puffer fish do not make good pets. However, if you enjoy fish and want a fish that will interact with you, then yes, puffer fish are extremely good pets.

Many aquarists find that puffer fish will come up to them when they are standing at the aquarium. They will wiggle, beg for food and will even play by spraying water out of the tank. This interaction is very rare with aquarium fish and most people who get one puffer fish often feel the need to get another.

Are they good fish for children to have?

Although puffer fish are entertaining, I do not recommend that you put any in an aquarium for children under the age of 12. Puffer fish do have toxins in their skin and spine and they can injure a child if they put their hands in the tank. In addition, puffer fish have very sharp teeth and strong jaws that can lead to severe damage if a child gets bitten.

Finally, puffer fish are hardy fish but they do require special care that a young child would not be able to provide.

Are they clean?

Well, puffer fish will not mess up your home but if you are looking for a clean aquarium dweller, then it is important to look for a different fish.

Puffer fish are predators and with predators comes a lot of mess with feeding. They often leave dead prey in the tank and this can make it hard to keep it clean. In addition, puffer fish need a wide range of food and this can mean making more mess in order to deal with their dietary needs.

Can they live in any aquarium?

Surprisingly, puffer fish are very versatile and there are actually species of puffer fish for every type of water. They can do very well in aquariums. That being said, however, puffer fish are not recommended for small tanks. They need at least 20 to 30 gallons and some species cannot be in aquariums that are smaller than 100 gallons.

Do you need special equipment for puffer fish?

With regards to equipment, you don't really need anything different for your puffer fish than what you would get for any fish. You will need a heater, filters, a good-sized aquarium and all of the other equipment necessary for setting up an aquarium. Read the chapter on setting up your aquarium to learn more about the equipment that you need.

What is the lifespan of a puffer fish?

The average lifespan of a puffer fish ranges depending on the species of puffer fish that you have purchased. Many puffer fish tend to live between 5 to 10 years.

Are there different types of puffer fish?

Yes, there are actually over 120 different types of puffer fish. They can also be found for freshwater aquariums, brackish water aquariums and marine, or saltwater, aquariums.

How big do puffer fish get?

Puffer fish vary in size depending on their species. Some do not grow much larger than an inch while others can reach up to 2 feet, or larger, in length.

How long do they take to mature?

Although puffer fish can live for 5 to 10 years, they do grow quickly. Many puffer fish are mature by 6 months of age; however, some are mature after two or three years.

The usual lifespan of a puffer fish begins with the puffer fish being hatched as larvae with a hard shell. By ten days of age, the larvae will begin a process of metamorphosis that sees them become a puffer fish by about 3 weeks after hatching. Most puffer fish can inflate themselves by 7 days after metamorphosis is complete.

Chapter 3. Snapshot of Puffer Fish Species

Although this book will go over the many tips for raising a puffer fish that is freshwater, saltwater or a combination of the two, there are many different species. In fact, there are so many different species that it is important to make some adjustments to how you care for them.

Later on in this book, I will go over the general care of the puffer fish but it is important to look at each species first. In this chapter, I will go over the popular species of puffer fish and give you a few facts that are important about those fish.

Remember that it is important to read the rest of the book on the fish to ensure that you provide everything that your puffer fish needs.

1. Marine Puffer Fish

The term marine refers to any fish that lives in salt water or oceans. They are found primarily in warm or tropic temperatures and are often found near and around coral reefs.

Marine puffer fish can range in size and they can be as small as 3mm long. Other species of puffer fish can grow up to 2 feet long. It is more common to keep the smaller sized fish in aquariums.

It is important to note that most marine puffer fish cannot be kept in aquariums with live coral. They commonly eat coral and will quickly destroy the coral in your tank.

Map Puffer Fish

A delightfully beautiful puffer fish, the Map Puffer, which is also known as the Scribbled Arothron Puffer or the Scribbled

15

Toadfish, has a brilliant display of colours. The base of the colouration is a light tan to dark yellow. Covering the body is a network of black markings that look very similar to the scribbles on a map.

This is a very large fish and it does need ample aquarium space. In addition to being able to grow to nearly 2 feet in length, it can puff itself up to almost double its size and the spines on the fish are held straight out. The fish does well in a tank with plants; however, it will eat coral so it may not be the best fish for a natural coral tank.

- *Tank Type:* Marine (salt water)
- *Minimum Tank Size:* 180 gal (682L)
- *Tank Ph:* 8.1 to 8.4
- *Salt Level:* sq. 1.020 to 1.025
- *Tank Temperature:* 72.0 to 78.0° F (22.2 to 25.6° C)
- *Personality:* Aggressive
- *Lifespan:* 15 years
- *Diet:* Carnivore
- *Adult Size:* 26 inches (66cm)
- *Ease of Care:* Medium Difficulty

Panda Puffer Fish

While its gets its name from the black patches of colour that surround both eyes, the Panda Puffer is also commonly known as the Masked Puffer. It is a beautiful marine puffer fish that should only be kept in marine aquariums.

The colouring of the Panda Puffer is a light grey that mixes with a bright white. The white is primarily found on the belly of the fish and parts of the head. A black mask around the eyes, as well as a black mark around the mouth and darker fins, creates a startling contrast of colour.

The Panda Puffer fish is another large fish and requires a large tank. In addition, it should only be kept in a fish only aquarium as it does eat coral.

- *Tank Type:* Marine (salt water)
- *Minimum Tank Size:* 100 gal (379L)
- *Tank Ph:* 8.1 to 8.4
- *Salt Level:* sq. 1.020 to 1.025
-*Tank Temperature:* 72.0 to 78.0° F (22.2 to 25.6° C)
- *Personality:* Semi-Aggressive
- *Lifespan:* 10 years
- *Diet:* Carnivore
-*Adult Size:* 12 inches (30cm)
- *Ease of Care:* Medium Difficulty

Porcupine Puffer Fish

With a name like porcupine, there probably isn't a lot that I need to go over as to their appearance. This is a popular puffer fish that is a light to dark brown in colour. The brown should fade down to the off-white belly.

On the entire fish there should be spines that stand straight out when the fish is startled. The Porcupine Puffer is a fairly large fish and it does need some room to grow. In addition, it is not the best fish to have many of, as it can live in a tank with fish that are the same or of a larger size than it. Be warned, however, that they will eat fish that are smaller.

- *Tank Type:* Marine (salt water)
- *Minimum Tank Size:* 100 gal (379L)
- *Tank Ph:* 8.1 to 8.4
- *Salt Level:* sq. 1.020 to 1.025
-*Tank Temperature:* 72.0 to 78.0° F (22.2 to 25.6° C)
- *Personality:* Calm
- *Lifespan:* 15 years
- *Diet:* Carnivore

-Adult Size: 11 inches (28cm)
- Ease of Care: Medium Difficulty

False-Eye Puffer Fish

The False-Eye Puffer is a small species of marine puffer fish. They are usually a brilliant orange in colour; however, they can be brown in colour as well. What makes them such a striking addition to a tank is the numerous bluish-green spots on the body and caudal fin.

In addition, black edged lines that are bluish green in colour extend slightly from the eyes, across the brow and there should be a black spot below the dorsal fins.

This is a beautiful fish that does very well in a community tank with a range of other fishes. Remember that most puffers will eat fish that are smaller than it and the False-Eye Puffer is no different.

- Tank Type: Marine (salt water)
- Minimum Tank Size: 30 gal (114L)
- Tank Ph: 8.1 to 8.4
- Salt Level: sq. 1.020 to 1.025
-Tank Temperature: 74.0 to 79.0° F (23.3 to 26.1° C)
- Personality: Calm
- Lifespan: Unknown
- Diet: Carnivore
-Adult Size: 5 inches (12cm)
- Ease of Care: Medium Difficulty

Striped Puffer Fish

The Striped Puffer Fish is a beautiful little fish that has a white to off-white body and vivid brown to black stripes that run down the length of the fish's body. They are another of the larger puffer fish and they do require a larger tank for the best health.

The Striped Puffer is not recommended for tanks with a large number of other fish. They are known as a fin nipper and will cause a lot of damage to other fish in the tank.

- *Tank Type:* Marine (salt water)
- *Minimum Tank Size:* 100 gal (379L)
- *Tank Ph:* 8.1 to 8.4
- *Salt Level:* sq. 1.020 to 1.025
-*Tank Temperature:* 74.0 to 79.0° F (23.3 to 26.1° C)
- *Personality:* Aggressive
- *Lifespan:* Unknown
- *Diet:* Carnivore
-*Adult Size:* 20 inches (50cm)
- *Ease of Care:* Medium Difficulty

2. Brackish Puffer Fish

Anyone who is new to the world of home aquariums is often unsure what the term brackish refers to. In simple terms, brackish is the section of a river that is a combination of both salt water and fresh water. It is commonly found where rivers empty out into the sea.

While many of the brackish puffers live primarily in the brackish water, it is important to note that they can survive in both fresh water and salt water. However, for the best health of your puffer, it is better to have them live in ideal brackish conditions, which I will go over later on in this book.

Brackish Puffer fish tend to be a bit smaller than other puffer fish species; however, there is one species that can grow up to close to 2 feet long. Because of their smaller size, they can be perfect for smaller tank set ups.

Brackish Puffer fish can be a bit difficult to take care of and are only recommended for aquarists who have intermediate to advanced skills in maintaining a tank.

Spotted Green Puffer Fish

The Spotted Green Puffer is an aggressive puffer fish that thrives in brackish waters, although they are commonly sold as a freshwater puffer. They are brilliantly coloured with rich green on the back and a white belly. The back is usually covered with darker green spots.

The body of the Spotted Green Puffer should be rounded with a stout appearance. There should be small spines on the back of the fish. The mouth should be small and the eyes should bulge slightly out of the forehead of the Spotted Green Puffer fish.

- *Tank Type:* Brackish, although they can do well in fresh water.
- *Minimum Tank Size:* 20 gal (75L)
- *Tank Ph:* 5.5 to 8.0
- *Tank Hardiness:* 5 to 20 ° dH
-*Tank Temperature:* 74.0 to 82.0° F (23.3 to 27.8° C)
- *Personality:* Aggressive
- *Lifespan:* 15 years
- *Diet:* Omnivore
-*Adult Size:* 6.7 inches (17.02cm)
- *Ease of Care:* Very Difficult

Amazon Puffer Fish

The Amazon Puffer Fish is also known as the "Bee Puffer" and the second name accurately describes its appearance. The fish has a golden coloured back that slowly fades into a white on its belly.

In addition to the golden colour, there are dark partial bands down the puffer fish's body, giving it that bumblebee look. The fish also has a large dark spot near the caudal fin and located on the underside of the fish.

The shape of the fish should be stout and rounded, however, it should have an almost bumblebee look to its shape.

- *Tank Type:* Brackish
- *Minimum Tank Size:* 15 gal (57L)
- *Tank Ph:* 5.5 to 8.0
- *Tank Hardiness:* 5 to 20 ° dH
- *Tank Temperature:* 72.0 to 82.0° F (22.2 to 27.8° C)
- *Personality:* Semi-aggressive
- *Lifespan:* 10 years
- *Diet:* Omnivore
- *Adult Size:* 3 to 5 inches (7 to 13cm)
- *Ease of Care:* Medium Difficulty

Pig-Nosed Puffer Fish

The Pig-Nosed Puffer is a stocky fish that has a stout shape to it. The head has a very distinct look and greatly resembles a pig as the nose of the puffer is turned up.

The fish has a grey back with green to yellow patterning on the back. The belly of the Pig Nosed Puffer should be white in colour.

With this fish, there is a very distinct patterning. On the head, there should be a black v that looks like an arrowhead. In addition, there should be two distinct circles on the flank of the body that resemble archery targets.

- *Tank Type:* Brackish
- *Minimum Tank Size:* 30 gal (114L)
- *Tank Ph:* 6.7 to 7.7
- *Tank Hardiness:* 5 to 15 ° dH
- *Tank Temperature:* 74.0 to 82.0° F (23.3 to 27.8° C)

- *Personality:* Aggressive
- *Lifespan:* 10 years
- *Diet:* Carnivore
-*Adult Size:* 6 inches (15cm)
- *Ease of Care:* Medium to Hard Difficulty

Fahaka Puffer Fish

Also known as the Band Puffer, this puffer fish is known for its horizontal bands of gold that run from the pectoral fins to the tail. In addition to that splash of colour, this brackish puffer fish has a brownish-grey back that fades into a white belly.

The shape of the Fahaka Puffer is elongated but it still has the characteristic stout shape that you expect to see in a puffer species.

The fish is covered in short prickles and it has the interesting ability to change its colour depending on its mood. The Fahaka Puffer also has bright red-orange eyes. This is a very large puffer that can grow over 18 inches in length.

- *Tank Type:* Brackish or Freshwater
- *Minimum Tank Size:* 125 gal (473L)
- *Tank Ph:* 5.5 to 8.0
- *Tank Hardiness:* 10 to 12 ° dH
-*Tank Temperature:* 75.0 to 82.0° F (23.9 to 27.8° C))
- *Personality:* Highly Aggressive
- *Lifespan:* 10 years
- *Diet:* Carnivore
-*Adult Size:* 18 inches (46cm)
- *Ease of Care:* Medium Difficulty

Malabar Puffer Fish

A very small species of puffer fish, the Malabar Puffer is one of the smallest puffer fish that you can find for your aquarium.

They are known for their slight size and their rounded body shape that looks similar to that of a bean with a tail.

Malabar Puffer Fish have a golden-brown back that fades into a yellow or white belly. They should have greenish-blue to black markings on their back and males should have a dark vertical line down the belly. Females, on the other hand, should not have this line but they should have a yellow belly as opposed to a white one.

This fish is known by several names including Dwarf Puffer and Blue Eyed Puffer. The former is due to its size while the latter is due to the distinct blue eyes that the fish has.

- *Tank Type:* Brackish or Freshwater
- *Minimum Tank Size:* 10 gal (38L)
- *Tank Ph:* 7.5 to 8.3
- *Tank Hardiness:* 8 to 15 ° dH
-*Tank Temperature:* 72.0 to 82.0° F (22.2 to 27.8° C)
- *Personality:* Aggressive
- *Lifespan:* 10 years
- *Diet:* Carnivore
-*Adult Size:* 1 inch (2.5cm)
- *Ease of Care:* Medium Difficulty

Golden Puffer Fish

If you are looking for a puffer with a slightly distinct and unusual appearance, then this is the puffer for you. While it is a puffer species, it does not have the trademarked body that you would expect from a puffer. Instead, the fish has an elongated body that is almost sleek in appearance.

In addition, the fish has an iridescent colouring to its scales that start with a golden-green back. The colour should fade into the golden-white belly and the eyes are usually a golden colour, hence its name.

The fins and tail of this puffer fish should be translucent. It is also commonly known as the Avocado Puffer Fish.

- *Tank Type:* Brackish
- *Minimum Tank Size:* 20 gal (76L)
- *Tank Ph:* 6.0 to 7.8
- *Tank Hardiness:* 4 to 18 ° dH
-*Tank Temperature:* 74.0 to 82.0° F (23.3 to 27.8° C)
- *Personality:* Aggressive
- *Lifespan:* 10 years
- *Diet:* Carnivore
-*Adult Size:* 4.5 inch (11cm)
- *Ease of Care:* Medium Difficulty

3. Freshwater Puffer Fish

Freshwater puffer fish are exactly as they are described, fish that live and thrive in fresh water. They are usually a fairly hardy species of fish that can do well in a range of tank sizes.

The fish are found in the wild throughout Asia and in parts of South America. Freshwater puffer fish can range in size; however, the majority of freshwater puffers are smaller in size.

It is important to note that there is a lot of controversy over many of the puffer fish species. Some feel that many freshwater puffers are really brackish water puffers while others feel that they are merely freshwater puffers. I find that many of the freshwater puffer fish can do well in both brackish and fresh water and it is up to the aquarist to decide.

Target Puffer Fish

Perfect for an aquarium with a high level of plant life, the Target Puffer is known as a lurker puffer, which means it stays motionless until its prey moves near it.

The fish is distinguished by its slightly elongated but stout body. In addition, the colours on this fish are distinct, with a spotted body that gives it the name Twin Spot Puffer as well as Target Puffer.

The colouring on the Target Puffer should be medium to dark brown on the back. The colour should fade into an off-white belly.

- *Tank Type:* Freshwater
- *Minimum Tank Size:* 30 gal (114L)
- *Tank Ph:* 6.5 to 7.5
- *Tank Hardiness:* 8 to 16 ° dH
- *Tank Temperature:* 75.0 to 82.0° F (23.9 to 27.8° C)
- *Personality:* Aggressive
- *Lifespan:* Unknown
- *Diet:* Carnivore
- *Adult Size:* 6 inch (15cm)
- *Ease of Care:* Easy to Medium Difficulty

Dwarf Puffer Fish

Also known as the Malabar Puffer, this is a fish that can be placed in either a freshwater tank or a brackish water tank. It is a very small species of puffer fish and is considered to be one of the smallest puffer fish that you can find for your aquarium. They are known for their slight size and the rounded body shape that looks similar to that of a bean with a tail.

Dwarf Puffer Fish have a golden-brown back that fades into a yellow or white belly. They should have greenish-blue to black markings on their back and males should have a dark vertical line down the belly. Females, on the other hand, should not have this line and they should have a yellow belly as opposed to a white one.

This fish is known by several names including Malabar Puffer.

- *Tank Type:* Freshwater or Brackish
- *Minimum Tank Size:* 10 gal (38L)
- *Tank Ph:* 7.5 to 8.3
- *Tank Hardiness:* 8 to 15 ° dH
- *Tank Temperature:* 72.0 to 82.0° F (22.2 to 27.8° C)
- *Personality:* Aggressive
- *Lifespan:* 10 years
- *Diet:* Carnivore
- *Adult Size:* 1 inch (2.5cm)
- *Ease of Care:* Medium Difficulty

Band Puffer Fish

Also known as the Fahakad Puffer, this puffer fish can be kept in both fresh water and brackish water. It is known for its horizontal bands of gold that run from the pectoral fins to the tail. In addition to that splash of colour, this brackish puffer fish has a brownish-grey back that fades into a white belly.

The shape of the Band Puffer is elongated but it still has the characteristic stout shape that you expect to see in a puffer species.

The fish is covered in short prickles and it has the interesting ability to change its colour depending on its mood. The Band Puffer also has bright red-orange eyes. This is a very large puffer that can grow over 18 inches in length.

- *Tank Type:* Freshwater or Brackish
- *Minimum Tank Size:* 125 gal (473L)
- *Tank Ph:* 5.5 to 8.0
- *Tank Hardiness:* 10 to 12 ° dH
- *Tank Temperature:* 75.0 to 82.0° F (23.9 to 27.8° C))
- *Personality:* Highly Aggressive
- *Lifespan:* 10 years

- *Diet:* Carnivore
-*Adult Size:* 18 inches (46cm)
- *Ease of Care:* Medium Difficulty

Brazilian Puffer Fish

If you are looking for a puffer fish that is fairly easy to care for and does well in community tanks, then this is the perfect one. It is actually a very peaceful puffer fish and is not overly aggressive, although it will bite fins.

It is characterized by its golden coloured back that slowly fades into a white on the belly.

In addition to the golden colour, there are dark partial bands down the puffer fish's body, giving it that bumblebee look. The fish also has a large dark spot near the caudal fin and located on the underside of the fish.

- *Tank Type:* Freshwater
- *Minimum Tank Size:* 30 gal (114L)
- *Tank Ph:* 6.5 to 7.5
- *Tank Hardiness:* 10 to 12 ° dH
-*Tank Temperature:* 75.0 to 82.0° F (23.9 to 27.8° C))
- *Personality:* Slightly Aggressive but calm
- *Lifespan:* 10 years
- *Diet:* Carnivore
-*Adult Size:* 6 inches (15cm)
- *Ease of Care:* Medium Difficulty

Figure Eight Puffer Fish

This beautiful little puffer fish is one of my personal favourites simply because of the beautiful markings that it has. The greyish fish has a dark back that fades into a white belly.

But despite that seemingly plain colouring, the Figure Eight Puffer has beautiful swirls of yellow surrounding darker spots of colour. The swirls give an almost figure eight look to the markings, hence the name Figure Eight.

This is a puffer fish species that is strictly a freshwater species and should not be placed in a brackish water tank.

- *Tank Type:* Freshwater
- *Minimum Tank Size:* 30 gal (114L)
- *Tank Ph:* 6.5 to 7.5
- *Tank Hardiness:* 5 to 12 ° dH
-*Tank Temperature:* 72.0 to 82.0° F (22.2 to 27.8° C)
- *Personality:* Slightly Aggressive
- *Lifespan:* 10 years
- *Diet:* Carnivore
-*Adult Size:* 3 inches (8cm)
- *Ease of Care:* Easy to Medium Difficulty

Mbu Puffer Fish

The final puffer fish species that we are going to look at in this chapter is the Mbu Puffer Fish. This is a strictly freshwater puffer fish that can grow to an enormous size. It is also one of the more popular puffer fish since they tend to have their own unique personalities.

The fish are characterized by a white belly and a patterned back of dark and light green and yellow patterns. The Mbu puffer fish often changes colour to match its mood and to also camouflage its body. One of the most unique aspects of this beautiful fish is the striped tail that it has. It usually keeps the tail folded but when it swims vigorously, it will fan it out.

- *Tank Type:* Freshwater
- *Minimum Tank Size:* 50 gal (189L) when young, 1000+ gal (3785L) when mature

28

- *Tank Ph:* 6.5 to 7.5
- *Tank Hardiness:* 10 to 15 ° dH
-*Tank Temperature:* 72.0 to 82.0° F (22.2 to 27.8° C)
- *Personality:* Aggressive
- *Lifespan:* 10 years
- *Diet:* Carnivore
-*Adult Size:* 24 inches (60cm)
- *Ease of Care:* Easy to Medium Difficulty

There are other types of puffers, roughly 120 different puffer fish
species that you can purchase, however, the ones that I have
listed are the most common ones that you will find. It is
important to note that many puffer fish have not been bred in
captivity and are still being taken from their natural habitat.
Make sure that you purchase from ethical suppliers. I have given
you a few links to ethical suppliers at the end of this book.

Chapter 4. Anatomy of a Puffer Fish

Now that you know about the different species of puffer fish available for your tank, I would like to take the time to go over the anatomy of a puffer fish. The main reason for this is simply because puffer fish are not like other fish. They have a few extra surprises for their owners, such as being able to puff their bodies up to nearly (and sometimes over) twice their body size.

In this chapter, I will go over the different parts of the puffer anatomy. Understanding the anatomy will help you in selecting your first puffer. In addition, it will help you to understand your puffer fish and know when it is not doing well in an environment.

In addition, through this chapter, I will go over the differences between male and female puffer fish and how you can determine it yourself.

1. Puffer Fish Anatomy

The first time that you see a puffer fish, you may not realize that there is anything different between them and the other fish in the tank. However, the first time that you see one puff up you will realize that there really are a lot of differences.

To start with, puffer fish are a very active fish that can provide their owners with a lot of entertainment. They have the amazing ability to hover in the water and this gives them an almost hummingbird like appearance. This is due to the assortment of fins and the placement of the fins.

7

a) Puffer Fish Gills

As you know, all fish have gills and the puffer fish does as well. However, they tend to be less noticeable than other fish so many owners are not aware of it when they are first purchase one.

The puffer fish should usually have gills that are open near their pectoral fins, usually right in front of it. The gills are usually very small and the opening of the gill looks more like a nostril opening than an actual gill.

The gill itself works in the same manner as all fish gills. A puffer fish breaths in a mouthful of water and then constricts its throat together. This forces the water out through the gills.

The gills themselves are filled with comb-like filaments called gill lamellae. These filaments enable the fish to remove oxygen from the water so they can breathe underwater. When you take a puffer fish out of the water, the gills will actually collapse. This is the reason why a fish cannot survive out of water so it is important to always transfer a puffer fish quickly.

b) Puffer Fish Nose

Yes, puffer fish have a nose but they are not like the nose on other animals. Like most fish, a puffer fish has nostrils or an olfactory pit, usually just above the mouth of the fish. However, the puffer fish usually has a slight extension from the nostril that is often seen as a strange adornment where the nostril should be.

One thing that should be noted is that while many puffer fish species have what looks like a nostril, they do not usually have any ability to smell. The main reason for this is because of the large jaws and teeth that puffer fish have. The development of these led to a very small olfactory system, hence their inability to smell or smell well.

All freshwater species are missing their olfactory pit or even the strange adornments, whilst many marine and brackish water species have the adornments near their nostrils.

c) Puffer Fish Fins

Puffer fish have several different fins that they use for manoeuvring around the tank. Although the fins do not seem to be too flexible and the puffer fish often looks clumsy, they are actually quite flexible.

Puffer fish are often very active and can swim with amazing speed and manoeuvrability. In addition, they have the ability to hover and this makes them a very interesting fish to watch.

Although there are several different fins on a puffer fish, it is interesting to note that the puffer fish does not have any pelvic fins, which are the two fins found on the bottom of a fish near the tail. Another interesting fact is the lack of this fin has not caused any issues in the mobility of the puffer fish.

With fins, every puffer fish should have:

Caudal Fin:

The caudal fin, or tail fin, can range in size on puffer fish. The tail is usually a truncate tail, which means that the tail has a square shape to it.

The tail fin is used primarily as a rudder to help the fish manoeuvre in a specific direction. However, they have been known to use the caudal fin to create a short burst of speed, particularly when they are hunting or escaping.

32

Dorsal Fin:

The dorsal fin is the fin that is found on the back of the puffer fish. Puffers can have either one or two dorsal fins and when there are two, they are very close together.

On a puffer fish, the dorsal fin is usually located close to the back of the fish – just before the tail begins. This fin is used for movement.

The dorsal fin of a puffer fish can be raised, lowered and it can also be undulated, which is moving them in a wave like motion.

Anal Fin:

This fin is exactly as it sounds, a fin that is found very close to the anus of the puffer fish. The anal fin is found behind the anus on the lower side of the fish.

Again, this fin is used for movement, although usually at a lesser extent. There should only be one fin.

Pectoral Fin:

The pectoral fins are fins that are found on either side of the puffer fish's body. They should be found directly behind the gills of the puffer fish and are usually fairly small. In fact, the pectoral fins appear nearly transparent.

The pectoral fins are one of the primary fins used for swimming. In fact, the pectoral fins are the main fins that give the puffer fish a hummingbird quality. By manipulating the fins, the puffer fish can hover, change direction by turning and flit around going forward, backward, up, down, left and right without any effort.

With fins, it is very important to always purchase a puffer fish that has all of its fins. While they can heal from having a torn or bitten fin, and the fin will grow back, they can die very easily when their fins are injured significantly.

d) Puffer Fish Body

The body of the puffer fish is another area that makes the fish unique. Although there are some differences in shape, most puffer fish have an almost football shape to them when they have not puffed themselves up.

In addition, most puffer fish have a stout body that makes them appear clumsy. It is important to note that despite the stout appearance, puffer fish can be very agile hunters.

The fish should have a broad head and many puffer fish species have a distinguishable brow, which gives them an almost human like appearance. There should also be a jaw line on a puffer fish.

The body of the puffer fish itself is not scaled and all puffer fish have spines, which I will go over in puffer fish defences, but many species do not have visible spines when they are not puffed up.

The skin of the puffer fish is usually brilliantly coloured and many puffer fish can change the colour of their skin. Puffer fish that can't change their colour can often change the intensity of their colours.

e) Puffer Fish Jaw and Teeth

As you know, puffer fish are known by many different names and are called a tetraodontidae, which refers to the teeth of the puffer fish. In fact, tetra means four.

The puffer fish has two upper teeth and two lower teeth that are actually fused together on each mandible. The teeth form a beak like structure in the mouth of the puffer fish.

In addition to the teeth, puffer fish have very strong jaws that make them an excellent predator. In fact, much of the way the puffer fish looks today, including the nostrils extended outside of the puffer fish's olfactory pit, is due to the development of the powerful jaws that they have. The jaws are necessary as puffer fish often feed on snails and other hard-shelled species.

Covering the puffer fish's teeth are fleshy lips. While they give the puffer fish a funny and very human like appearance, the lips are used for tasting and touch. While the puffer fish is eating, the lips send signals to the brain to let the puffer fish known whether the food is worth eating or not.

Another interesting fact about the puffer fish's mouth is that it can squirt water out from between the lips. This is often used to move sand from the floor of the tank or the ocean floor while it is searching for food. Many owners, however, have found that puffer fish will also squirt the water out at the surface of the tank and will spray water up at their owners.

One thing that is very important with puffer fish care is to maintain the teeth through diet. If it is not maintained with a proper diet, the puffer fish's teeth will continue to grow and will not be ground down. After they reach a certain length, the puffer fish will not be able to eat and will starve to death. For more on puffer fish teeth care, read the chapter on caring for your puffer fish.

f) Puffer Fish Eyes

The eyes of the puffer fish are a true representation of a hunting animal that relies on eyesight to find food. While many fish have stationary eyes, the puffer fish has eyes that can be moved independently. This means that the puffer fish has the ability to search around for food, while many other species of fish have to lurk and wait for food to come within sight.

In addition to the ability to move on their own, the puffer fish's eyes also have the ability to lock onto a target and create a binocular vision. This enables them to grab their prey much easier than it does if the eyes could not be moved into a forward position.

The eyes of the puffer fish are set wide apart, almost on either side of the head, and they lie outside of the fish and not inside, hence the ability to move them in multiple directions.

Another trait of the puffer fish is that many puffer fish species have a bluish-green iridescence on their corneas. At this point, there is no known reason for the colouration but it is believed to help control the amount of light that enters the eyes.

2. Puffer Fish Defences

When it comes to defence, the puffer fish has a surprising list of instruments at its disposal. Many of these things can be talked about in the section on anatomy but they are so unique that it is better to talk about defence on its own.

a) Puff Defence

When it comes to reasons to purchase a puffer fish, the ability to puff up is often the main one. It is what makes a puffer fish a puffer fish and it is an interesting ability that only fish belonging to the tetraodontiformes, to which the puffer fish belongs, are able to do.

The puffer fish is able to expand its body to several times its full size. The fish does this by drawing water into its body through its mouth.

When it has a mouthful of water, there is an oral valve that moves forward to the front of the puffer fish's mouth to create a tight seal. This prevents any water from escaping from between the lips of the puffer fish.

When the mouth is sealed, a "plunger" type gill, called a branchiostegal ray, is used to draw the water down the esophagus and into the stomach.

This enables the puffer fish to expand since it is expanding with water. The actual body and stomach of the puffer fish have a ribbed membrane that allows the stomach and skin to stretch to enormous extents. In fact, some fish can balloon up to over a 100 times their actual size.

Puffer fish are able to expand in this manner because they do not have any ribs or pelvic bones. This enables their body to expand quickly and without hindrance. To prevent expanding too much, the puffer fish has set muscles that stop the expansion when it has reached the maximum.

When it feels safe enough to deflate, the puffer fish releases the water through its gills and also through its mouth.

Puffer fish use the puff defence whenever they are frightened or feeling agitated in any way. It is an excellent defence as it keeps predators from being able to swallow it. One interesting fact is that when it is inflated, the puffer fish's skin is so tough that it can deflect the bites of other predators.

b) Toxin

I am sure everyone has heard of the sushi dish called Fugu and the notoriety that surrounds it. Fugu is raw puffer fish and while it can be an exciting delicacy, it is one that is fraught with danger.

In addition to the ability to inflate its body, the puffer fish also has a secondary defence through strong neurotoxins. These neurotoxins can be found on the skin of the puffer fish, although not all species have the toxin on their skin. In addition, it is commonly found in the ovaries and the liver of the fish. Lastly, the neurotoxin can be found, in lower amounts, in the muscles of the fish.

The neurotoxin that is found in puffer fish is called Tetrodotoxin. It is highly toxic and it can cause death within a matter of hours. There is no known antidote for the tetrodotoxin and it can be deadly. In fact, tetrodotoxin has been linked to 100 deaths per year. In fact, tetrodotoxin is so strong that even a few milligrams can cause death and it is known to be deadly to 60% of people who consume the toxin.

Thankfully, those deaths are due to the fish being eaten so it is not something that most aquarists have to worry about. In addition, there are a number of puffer fish species that do not have toxin. One thing every aquarist should consider is the community that they place their puffer fish in. If there is a larger predator in the tank, you could create a scenario where you lose both fish.

c) Colour Change

I have already mentioned this but some species of puffer fish are able to change their colours. While this can be used for a number of reasons, many scientists believe that they use it to camouflage themselves with the surrounding terrain.

The puffer fish can use the camouflage for both hunting and for escaping from predators. There has also been some indication that they will change colours to reflect their mood.

c) Spines

The last defence that your puffer fish has is spines. It is important to note that all puffer fish have spines, although you may not be aware of it until your fish inflates its body.

When the puffer fish inflates its body, spines that have been hidden in the body of the puffer fish extend and stand straight out. This makes it very difficult for a predator to eat the puffer fish.

In addition, the spines of the puffer fish are often coated in a neurotoxin and this can poison any animal that is trying to eat it.

Once the puffer fish deflates, the spines are once again hidden in the body of the fish. It is important to note that not all puffer fish have toxin on their spines but all puffer fish have spines. The porcupine puffer fish is one of the few that have visible spines when it is not inflated.

3. Sexing a Puffer Fish

The final section on anatomy is one that is actually shrouded in mystery. Generally, when you are looking for a male or female puffer fish, you are going to have a very difficult time of it. As far as most people know, there is very little to help you determine the difference between a male and a female.

In fact, some species seem to have no apparent differences between the two. In addition, most puffer fish are sold as juveniles, which are young, teenaged puffer fish. During the juvenile stage, there are no discernible differences.

When it comes to temperament and personality, the same can be said. Usually, a puffer fish has a personality that is unique to itself. In addition, males are no more aggressive or no less aggressive than females.

Still, if you are trying to determine whether your puffer fish is male or female, there are a few things that you can look for, depending on the species.

- Bright Colours: Bright colours are often an indication that the puffer fish is a male. Generally, they are only slightly brighter but again, this is not a hard rule and some brightly coloured puffer fish can be female.

- More Brown: Another theory on indicating gender is that females tend to have browner colouration on them. Again, this is not always seen and some species have no brown on them at all.

- Less Green: Another indication that a puffer fish is female is the lack of green colouration on the fish. Usually, females that have green colouration have less than males from the same species but again; this is by no means a rule.

- Stripe down the Belly: Finally, there is a puffer fish whose sex you can determine very easily, but only when it is an adult. This is the Dwarf Puffer Fish. When it is an adult, males have a line or a row of spots running down its belly. Females do not have this line.

When you are trying to choose a puffer fish according to gender, it can be next to impossible. Remember, whether you get male or female is really just the luck of the draw.

Chapter 5. The Puffer Fish Personality

When you first tell a person new to fish that puffer fish, and really many other types of fish, have personalities, they often look at you like you are crazy. However, as they build their own aquarium community, they start to realize that all of their fish do, in fact, have personalities.

Puffer fish are some of the best fish to have around if you are looking for a personality. While they have a very expressive face, they also match that face with some interesting personality quirks. In fact, many aquarists will talk about how their puffer fish know who their owners are and will react and interact to them.

As mentioned in the last chapter, puffer fish have very expressive faces. This is due to the large eyes that can move in various directions. While it can make them cute and clown like, it can also give the appearance of a human face when the puffer fish is focusing both eyes forward. Combing these physical traits with apparent personality traits has made for a winning combination that any fish enthusiast will want.

It is important, when you are planning your aquarium in the next chapter, to think about the personality that your puffer fish will have. As you can guess, a tank that is designed improperly, with very little for the puffer fish to do, will lead to your puffer fish becoming bored, which will affect his personality.

In this chapter, I will go over everything that you need to know about your puffer fish's personality and traits that make the puffer fish unique.

1. The Hunter

One of the very first things that I tell anyone interested in adding a puffer fish to their aquarium is that puffer fish are hunters. Although there are many species that are omnivores, the majority of puffer fish are primarily carnivores. None are herbivores.

What this means is that any time that you have a puffer fish in your tank, you are basically introducing a predator into your aquarium.

If you are only keeping puffer fish in your aquarium, then this is not a huge problem. In fact, if the puffer fish is the only fish in the tank, then you really don't have to worry about the predator personality, until it is time to feed the fish.

However, if you are planning on keeping other fish in the tank with your puffer, there are a few things that you should remember.

1. Puffer fish will eat just about anything. They aren't shy about what they eat and many will eat plants, other fish's fins and even decorative coral. In fact, many puffer fish will destroy any coral that is in the tank.

2. Smaller fish are excellent prey. Even if a fish isn't on their natural menu, if it is smaller than the puffer fish, there is a very high chance that the puffer fish will eat it. In the event that the fish are larger, you may find fins nibbled off of your other fish.

3. Other predators are competition. Since it is a hunter, puffer fish will often attack any other predators that it feels competes with it for food. I would strongly recommend having a limited number of strong predators in your tank as they may fight.

4. Puffer fish learn where the food is. The final point with a puffer fish hunter is that they know where the food is and learn to accept you as the feeder. In fact, if you always feed from a feeding rod, the puffer fish will learn to swim up to you at mealtime. While some are wonderful hunters, many puffer fish are opportunistic and if a meal is to be had easily, they will take it.

When it comes to the hunting puffer fish, it is surprising to learn that there are different personalities with the hunters. Some hunt according to the type of puffer fish species it is but other puffer fish adapt to their tank. If it is a species known to hide and lurk in the wild and there is nowhere for it to lurk and hide, then it will adapt and change its hunting pattern.

There are actually three different types of hunters that you can have in a puffer fish and each one has a very unique personality.

a) Open Water Hunters

These are wonderfully energetic and active fish since they are used to looking for their food. They will often swim around the tank and you can tell that they are usually searching for food amongst the aquarium's decorations.

Generally, they will search plants, substrate and even in the crevices of the decorations. Its energetic personality makes it more interesting to watch. It also has a very efficient manner of hunting and will often catch prey that seems unobtainable.

With open water hunter puffer fish, it is important to remember that this is a fish that is going to have a large section of the tank as his territory. The fish will often be a bit more aggressive to other fish that swim in his way and this can lead to problems in your fish community.

Even with the challenges, the careful, efficient hunter that you find in open water hunters is an interesting fish to have in your tank. One thing to point out is that a vast majority of puffer fish are open water hunters.

Another fact that every aquarist should know is that even though they are open water hunters, they should not have only open water. This is a fish that loves to search out its prey. If there are no crevices, tangles of plants or obstacles, the open water hunter will quickly become bored.

Give the puffer fish plenty of things to search through and also give him expanses of open water so he can search through patches of substrate for his food.

b) Ambush Hunters

Slow, patient and one of the best puffer fish for connecting with their owners, the ambush hunter is a puffer fish that finds a place to burrow in and wait. These are the fish that aren't overly active and will spend much of their time burrowed under the substrate or hiding in a crevice.

However, once food passes by, there is often a burst of energy that is always startling. The ambush hunters are as efficient with its form of hunting as the open water hunter so you shouldn't avoid this fish simply because it is not always swimming.

As I mentioned, the ambush hunter puffer fish is a very slow fish but they do enjoy getting their food handed to them. This makes them a very easy fish to train to a feeding rod since the puffer fish enjoy having you bring the food to them.

In addition, this type of puffer fish doesn't need to be fed live food. If you simply place the food on a feeding rod and dangle it in the water, the ambush puffer fish will eat it. This makes care a bit easier.

With ambush hunters, you want to make sure that your aquarium has loose sand covering the bottom. Don't use heavy gravel or rocks since it can lead to sores on your puffer fish's body. Make sure any decorations you have do not have any holes that your ambush hunter can get stuck in. Remember, you want the fish to be able to hide but you want to be able to still enjoy your fish so don't make the hiding spots so good that you can't see him.

c) Stealth Hunters

The final type of hunters that you will usually see in your puffer fish is the stealth hunter. This is a fish that likes to stay close to where they can hide but they don't hunt primarily as an ambush hunter. Instead, they use a variety of hunting techniques such as searching for food and lurking to get their meals.

Stealth hunters are usually a more timid puffer fish. They are not as confident as the open water hunters that will cruise around the aquarium like they own it. Instead, they tend to be a bit nervous and will quickly dart into hiding as soon as a "predator," including their owners, comes into sight.

Because of this, it can be very difficult for owners to really get a feel for their puffer fish's personality. They tend to take a bit longer to train to hand feeding because of this temperament but once they are, they are usually a very interesting and personable puffer fish.

Generally, stealth hunters are smaller species of puffer fish. They have developed the stealth hunting technique to allow them to search for food while still being in reach of safety. One of the most interesting points with the stealth hunter is that it is usually very easy to determine males from females.

Females tend to hang back a bit more and are less likely to move out into the open for hunting. In addition, females that are in species known for being stealth hunters usually have muted colours while males have brighter colours.

With regards to tank set up for a stealth hunter, you want to have a range of hiding places and open spaces. You want the puffer fish to feel secure when it is out searching for food so you don't want to make the open spaces too open. Remember, if the fish can get to shelter easily, it will venture out more frequently.

2. Puffer Fish Personality

While the type of hunter your puffer fish is will affect his personality, anyone who has ever owned his or her own puffer fish knows that there is more to the personality than simply hunting. In fact, puffer fish are very personable and this is the main attraction of keeping them in an aquarium.

For the most part, your puffer fish will have a very unique personality. This is something that you will see right away but as you encourage interactions with your puffer fish you will begin to see differences in the personality.

Many puffer fish are very playful. They will often swim up when they see their owners and will wiggle around in the water in front of them. In addition, some will play games such as squirting their owners with water.

Another personality trait that is shared amongst puffer fish is the fish's ability to be very focused. Many aquarists have found that their puffer fish will come up and focus on them when they are talking to the fish. In addition, there have even been reports of puffer fish watching television.

These traits often make puffer fish seem very human-like and their personalities are as varied as the puffer fish species out there.

3. Negative Personality Traits

The final points that I want to go over in regards to your puffer fish's personality is the negative personality traits that can occur in your puffer fish from time to time. Remember, these are predatory fish so they will have a higher level of aggression and territorial impulses.

a) The Fin Nipper

The fin nipper is a puffer fish that is just that, a fin nipper. While most people look at this as a normal occurrence with puffer fish, it is important to note that some fish can become obsessed with fin nipping.

For some puffer fish, this fin nipping is very common and it can be something they do as a supplement to their regular diet. They can be almost parasitic when they are fin nipping for food and it is not something that you want to encourage. Keeping ample food for your puffer fish can help cut down on this, as can keeping faster swimming fish.

Fin nippers are often created simply because the puffer fish is a thug. This is often caused by severe aggression in the puffer fish, which we will go over in the next section, or due to boredom. When the puffer fish has this aggression, he will attack the fish that come into his territory. If it is a small tank, you are more likely to see this type of aggression. However, it can simply be the species that is overly aggressive.

With fin nipping, it is important to follow a few tips to help stave off the habit. These are:

48

- Fast swimming fish. I have already mentioned this but having faster swimming fish in your tank can discourage fin nipping. Puffer fish usually prey on slower fish since they tend to be slow moving themselves. However, this is not always the case so still keep an eye on your puffer to make sure that he is not a fin nipper.

- Keep the puffer fish fed. As I have mentioned, many puffer fish will eat fins as a supplement to their diet. The best way to prevent this is to keep the puffer fish fed. In addition, make sure that it has a well-rounded diet, which I have gone over in the chapter on diet.

- Give them stimulation. Finally, give your puffer fish things to explore. If there is nothing in the tank, you will see more aggression and more boredom from the puffer fish. The more space in the tank the more fin nipping will occur.

In the end, however, you should be prepared for some puffer fish that cannot be rehabilitated and will continue to nip fins. In these cases, you may have to choose a tank where the puffer fish is the only inhabitant.

b) The Aggressor

One of the most shocking things that you can see with your puffer fish is when it is extremely aggressive. There doesn't seem to be any rhyme or reason for the aggression but the puffer fish spends much of its time attacking other fish in the tank.

In addition, when you remove the other fish from the tank, the fish continues to attack things, including the plants that are in the aquarium. When they feed, it tends to be very aggressive, more so than what is usual.

Although it may seem as though the puffer fish is defunct in some way, this is not the case. All puffer fish are prone to aggression but some species have a higher chance of being aggressive. The very first thing that you should do is make sure that you have not purchased a puffer fish species that has a high aggression level.

The second thing that you should do is make sure that your puffer fish has everything that it needs. It is very common for puffer fish to become aggressive when they are bored.

In addition, if a puffer fish does not have a lot of food, he may begin to become territorial over the food that is in the tank. This means that he may also attack fish that are not really a threat to his food supply.

Generally, puffer fish that become aggressive and territorial over feeding grounds do so with food that is not easily replaced. Clams, snails and other food that grows slowly can become a territorial food for the puffer fish. The best way to prevent this territorial food guarding is by having plenty of food in the tank for your puffer fish.

Another time that you may see high levels of aggression is if you are breeding your puffer fish. Many species protect their eggs and it is the job of the male to do this. Generally, this form of aggression only occurs in males during certain times of the year: mating and nesting seasons. The males in the tank will begin to protect an area that is suitable for a nest and if you have more than one male and a female in the tank, you will see aggression when it comes time to breed.

Lastly, aggression often occurs because of the size of the aquarium. If there are a large number of fish in the tank, the puffer fish will become aggressive in an effort to hold on to his territory.

Likewise, if the tank is too small, you will notice more aggression from your puffer fish. In addition, there is less room for your puffer fish and other fish to coexist peacefully. Even for species that can survive in a smaller tank, I always recommend that you try to have a tank that is 55 gallons at the smallest.

c) The Bored Fish

One problem that often occurs in a puffer fish is boredom. Although there is a lot of debate on whether puffer fish are intelligent or not, no one argues that puffer fish can become bored. It is very common and is usually symptomatic of the tank setup.

Puffer fish that are bored often display a lot of different behaviour. Some can become fin nippers as I have mentioned, and others can become very aggressive. Some puffer fish may seem almost depressed and may begin to ignore food.

Another behaviour that occurs with boredom is glass swimming. This is where the puffer fish will continually go up and down the glass. While it is not usually harmful, some puffer fish have been known to exhaust themselves with this behaviour. In addition, they may not eat.

With boredom, the main and only way to combat it or to prevent it is to have things in the tank for your puffer fish to search through. This is very important for tanks that have open water hunters since our first reaction is to put in very little decoration. Ways to prevent boredom are:

- *Sand as a substrate.* Although you can use rocks and other substrates, almost all puffer fish love sand. It gives them something to do and search through and they seem to enjoy the feeling of the sand on their skin.

- Use a variety of plants. This is very good for puffer fish that are open water hunters since this will give them a number of places to search for food. Plants that are floating are excellent for open water hunters since this will let them search both on the substrate and up near the top of the water.

- Have caves for the puffer fish. Another thing that you can place in the aquarium is decorations that give the puffer fish caves. They love to search through them for food and they also use them to hide in. It is important to make sure that your puffer fish will be able to swim in the cave without getting stuck.

- Interesting decorations. Finally, have a range of interesting decorations in your fish tank. This can be natural wood or plastic decorations but the key is to have a variety of items for the puffer fish to explore.

Generally. the rule of thumb is to have a variety of things for your puffer fish to do and "play" with. The more complex the habitat, the happier your puffer fish will be. The happier your puffer fish is, the less likely you will see boredom and other negative personality quirks.

Chapter 6. Preparing for your Puffer Fish

Now that you know as much as you can about the species of puffer fish available and the anatomy of a puffer fish, it is time to start setting up your tank.

As I have mentioned many times throughout this book, there are actually several different types of puffer fish and they all need specific care associated with the type they are. Marine puffer fish cannot survive in freshwater or brackish water tanks while freshwater puffer fish cannot survive in marine or saltwater tanks.

It is imperative that you choose the right tank and the right levels for your puffer fish to make sure that it has everything it needs to survive.

1. Your Aquarium

The first thing that I would like to touch on with preparing for your puffer fish is how to set up your tank. This is usually the most important thing that you should have set up before hand. Later on in this chapter I will go over each individual tank that you should have depending on your species, but for now, I want to touch on the tank in general.

Firstly, you should consider the size of your aquarium. Remember that many species of puffer fish can grow quite large. In fact, some puffer fish species can grow to be up to 2 feet in length.

In addition, puffer fish can be extremely territorial. If you want to have more than one puffer fish in your tank, you are going to have to have enough room to keep them out of each other's way. It is important to note, however, that puffers are not always going to do well in a tank together.

Although the size of tank will vary depending on the species of puffer fish that you purchase, a good rule of thumb is to have 20 gallons or 75 litres per puffer fish. This is the minimum amount, but for species that are much larger you will need to have a higher minimum.

One thing that has been observed by many aquarists is that the more space you have for your puffer the better, especially if you are keeping more than one fish in your tank.

In addition to size, you need to consider what type of material your tank will be made of. In today's market, there are a lot of different materials from plastics to glass and it really is up to you what you want to have your tank made of.

For puffer fish, I do not recommend any plastic fish tanks as the majority of plastic tanks are small tanks designed for one or two small fish such as goldfish or a beta.

With that in mind, you are really only left with two different types of tanks – glass and Plexiglas.

Glass Aquariums:

Glass is often the go to choice for anyone who is interested in starting a fish tank. They can be found in a number of different sizes and they are usually of high quality. The glass is tempered to withstand the weight of water in a filled tank.

In addition, glass usually has a clearer view into the fish tank and is less prone to scratches when you are cleaning it. On the down side, glass is usually very heavy and very expensive. In addition, you can only purchase a square or bowed glass tank and this keeps you from having an interesting tank shape.

Lastly, glass can be broken very easily and there is always the risk of that occurring.

Plexiglas Aquariums:

Plexiglas aquariums have come a long way and have nearly caught up with glass when it comes to quality. While they tend to be a bit cloudy when you are trying to view the fish, if you purchase a high quality Plexiglas, you won't be able to notice it.

There are actually a number of benefits when it comes to Plexiglas. First, it can be shaped into any design that you want, which can make an interesting art piece for your tank. In addition, it is more durable and sturdy than glass and it is not as heavy or expensive.

On the down side, Plexiglas is not as clear as glass and it is more difficult to clean. Lastly, Plexiglas tends to scratch much easier than a glass aquarium and you will quickly notice the wear and tear on the tank.

When it comes to tanks, I recommend glass. They are worth the added expense because glass gives you the best view of your fish.

The very last thing that you should consider with your tank is what you want it for. Are you housing just one fish or did you want to create a community? If you are going to house one fish, you can keep your tank to a minimum and you will not need a lot of space. If you want to create a community, you are going to need a large aquarium and it is important that you have the space for it.

a) Setting up an Aquarium

As you know, there are several species of puffer fish that survive in fresh water, brackish water and salt water and this gives you a lot of options for your aquarium. Setting up a tank does not have to be difficult; however, there are a few things that you should remember to do:

1. Always clean the tank thoroughly before you add anything into it. If it is an old tank, it should be disinfected to ensure that there is no disease present in the tank. If it is new, it should still receive a thorough cleaning.

When you are cleaning a tank, make sure that you do not use harsh chemicals as the residue can stay in the tank and poison your fish.

2. Always check for leaks. This should be done regardless of the age or the number of uses. Occasionally, a seal may be broken on a brand new tank and it doesn't become apparent until you have it filled.

Fill the tank with water and allow it to sit for a few days to make sure that there are no leaks. Don't bother doing anything else with the tank until you know if there is a leak or not.

3. Clean everything that is going into the tank. Whether it is a decoration, a filter or a plastic plant, you should clean the items. Remember, if they are old pieces of equipment, there could be disease on them. If they are new, you should still wash them to ensure there are no residues on the items.

Cleaning is very important when you are setting up any new tank as this will help ensure that nothing is getting into your tank that you don't want.

2. Setting up a Freshwater Tank

As I have mentioned, there are actually several ways that you can set up your aquarium, as there are several different species. Freshwater tanks are often considered to be a great place to start and there are many species of puffer fish that can thrive in fresh water.

One thing that I should point out is that a freshwater tank does not meant that it will be easy to care for. While many aquarists start in the world of freshwater tanks, there are many things that you should be aware of.

As you know, to have the most success from your aquarium, it is important to make sure that you are starting off on the right foot. This section will teach you everything that you need to know about setting up your tank for your puffer fish. Make sure that you check your specific puffer fish breed to determine what the fish needs.

a) Equipment

When it comes to a tank, it is often the supplies that can make it successful or not. While you may be looking to save money on your equipment, I strongly recommend that you do not go with the cheaper options. Remember, you get what you pay for and the quality of the equipment can affect the quality of life for your fish.

Equipment and supplies that are an absolute must have for your freshwater tank set up are:

- Filter: Having a good filter is very important for your fish. There are many different filters out there, but I recommend that you use an Aquaclear or a Marineland filter. They are usually of very high quality and they don't break down as quickly as other filters.

With filters, I strongly recommend that you purchase the right filter for the size of your tank. A 50-gallon tank should not have a filter for a 20-gallon tank. In addition, make sure that you use two filters in your tank. The reason for this is twofold. Firstly, your tank will be cleaner. Secondly, you will always have a backup filter running if one filter fails.

- Heater: As you know, puffer fish live in tropical climates. This means that they do require warm water to survive properly. Again, temperature will vary depending on the species of puffer fish that you are putting in the tank. With heaters, I recommend Marineland heaters. They are usually very durable and are perfect for getting the temperature right.

As with filters, I recommend that you use two heaters. The main difference is that you should use smaller heaters instead of one designed for your tank size. For instance, if you have a 100-gallon tank, choose two 50-gallon heaters. Make sure you set them up on either side of the tank to help heat the water thoroughly. The nice thing with having two heaters is that you will find the water stays a more even temperature and if a heater dies, you will have the backup running.

- Thermometer: As with all tanks that have to be heated, always make sure that you have a thermometer in your tank to determine the temperature of the water. Make sure that you check it frequently and make sure that the temperature stays in the ideal range. If there is a rise or drop in temperature, it could lead to shock, disease and even death for your puffer fish.

- Lid: There are different types of lids and aquarium hoods that you can purchase for your tank but it is important to have one. Some, if not all, species of puffer fish can jump out of the water and it is not uncommon for them to do so. The lid will keep your puffer fish from getting out.

Another benefit of a lid of some kind is that it will keep contaminants out of your tank. Air fresheners, dust, and other outside contaminants can land in the water. Even minute traces of some contaminants can destroy the ecosystem in your tank and make your fish sick.

- Substrate: There are many different types of substrate, which is the sand, gravel or rocks that line the bottom of an aquarium, which you can purchase. Really, it is up to the effect that you are going for.

What you want to consider with substrate is your puffer fish species. Some species prefer to burrow into the substrate. If this is the case, you want to avoid a heavy substrate as they can cause injury to themselves when burrowing. Sand is the best option for a puffer fish that burrows.

If you have a species that is not known to burrow, you can use any type of substrate, however, you want to find one that is aquarium safe. In addition, only use substrate that is smooth to help prevent any damage to your fish.

- Tank Vacuum: There are many different types of tank vacuums that you can use and it is really up to you. I prefer to use a tank python but you can purchase higher quality tank vacuums.

- Aquarium Gloves: Finally, make sure that you purchase a good pair of aquarium gloves. This will enable you to place your hands into the aquarium without the worry of contamination from your skin. In addition, aquarium gloves allow you to handle the fish in your aquarium safely.

b) Decorations

Although decorations can be viewed as equipment for your aquarium, I feel it is important to look at it separately to ensure that you have the right set up for your fish. Puffer fish need a range of decorations for both hiding and to keep them entertained. Many people do not realize it but fish can become bored.

- Plants: Plants are often debated when it comes to puffer fish for one reason: many puffer fish will bite the plants in their tank and

this will lead to dead plants and an unsightly tank. On the other hand, puffer fish do enjoy having places to hide. When it comes to my own tanks, I side with having plants. It makes the tank look nicer and if you choose properly, you don't really have to worry about the nipping.

Firstly, it is important to decide on whether you will have fake or real plants. There are pros and cons for both and today, fake plants can look as nice as a real plant.

If you are going with fake, I strongly recommend that you choose silk plants instead of plastic. The reason for this is that they have a more lifelike appearance to them. Another reason is that they tend to be easier to weigh down, which will prevent them from floating to the surface.

If you are going with live plants, I recommend that you choose plants that have a thick root system and a broad leaf. This will help prevent the puffer fish from uprooting your plants. In addition, it will keep your fish from biting your plants in half.

- Regular Tank Decorations: Tank decorations are usually very common in all aquariums, regardless of the type of fish you keep. Puffer fish tanks are really no different and you can place anything that you want in the tank. Make sure that any decorations in the tank are free of sharp edges as puffer fish will rub against these things and cut their skin.

In addition, make sure that there are no small holes where the fish will get stuck. You do want to have caves in the tank but you want to make sure that the fish can swim out of those caves easily.

- Natural Terrain: The last way to decorate your tank is with natural terrain. Logs, rocks, and large shells can be a nice decoration in the tank. In addition, puffer fish usually enjoy

exploring these natural elements in the tank and it will help with problems such as boredom and aggression.

Be inventive with what you place in your tank but make sure that it is safe for fish. In addition, make sure that you clean anything before you put it in your tank.

c) Chemicals

When it comes to chemicals in a fish tank, there is actually a large list of them that you can use. However, I am not going to give you that list because they do nothing for your fish in the long run.

Instead, they often cause you to have unnecessary expenses and they can be harmful to your fish if you are not using them properly.

The only thing that I recommend you purchase for the water in your tank at this point is water testing strips or a water testing kit. If you go back to the chapter on the puffer fish species that you can purchase, you will notice things such as pH. Test strips will help you test the levels in your water to ensure that is ideal for your puffer fish.

You can purchase chemicals to rise and lower the levels as needed; however, I strongly recommend that you cycle your tank instead of adding the chemicals. It does take longer but it will ensure that your tank has ideal conditions without a lot of added cost. I will go over cycling your tank in the next section on actually setting up the aquarium.

d) Getting your Tank Ready

Now that you know the various items that you have to have for your fish tank, it is time to start getting it ready. As I have already mentioned, it is very important to wash everything that you are placing into your aquarium. This will help prevent contamination from outside contaminants.

Once you have everything washed, it is time to start setting up your tank. This is not something that I can really guide you through. Read the instructions on any equipment that you have and install it as directed.

Next, do a dry run of how you would like your tank set up. I place the items where I want them and then add the substrate. If an item should be buried slightly under the substrate, then I do this, if not, I pick up the items, pour the substrate under the item and then place it on top.

If you are putting in plants, it is best to wait until you have the water in the tank as some plants need the water to keep from flattening; this is often the case with live plants.

Once you have everything set up, you can begin pouring in the water. The best way to do this is to place a flat dish in the centre of your aquarium and pour the water into the dish so that it runs off the dish. You can also run a hose into the tank and have the water slide down the glass of the aquarium. You do not want a steady stream of water going into the substrate as this will cause the substrate to float in the tank and the water may become cloudy.

When you have the tank filled, you can begin to run your filters and also run your heaters. You want the water to sit for 1 to 2 days before you add any fish. This will ensure that the chlorine is out of the water without having to use a dechlorinating chemical.

After the one or two days, check the temperature of the tank until you get it to the right temperature. When it is at the right temperature, you can begin to cycle your tank, which is how you get the ph levels to the right stage.

Really, when it comes to setting up your tank, all you need to do is put in the equipment, add the water and then do a cycling. Cycling does take time and I will go over the steps you need to take in the next section.

e) Cycling your Tank

As I have mentioned, there is a way to get your tank chemicals to the right level without having to use chemicals in your fish tank. This process does take a bit longer than chemicals and you will not be able to add a puffer fish to your tank until after 30 days.

To properly cycle your tank, there are a few steps that you should take.

Step One: Fill the Tank

As I have already mentioned, fill the tank with water. You can use filtered water but I find it is less expensive and more practical to use tap water. Once it is full, allow it to sit for a few days until the chlorine has been removed. This is very important before you move to the next stage of cycling.

Step Two: Add in a Few Fish

The next step that you should take is to add a few fish to your tank. It is important that you choose some cheaper fish from the pet store. Generally, cheap fish are mass-produced and kept in conditions that are less than ideal. Because of this, they tend to be hardier fish.

Fish that you can use are large tetras or small barbs. You want to make sure that they are known as a hardy fish since the conditions in your tank are going to get very poor as you are going through the cycling process.

Add the fish according to the species and the gallons. You want to have a good number of fish but not too many that the tank is overpopulated.

Step Three: Test the Water Daily

Make sure you test the water levels on a daily basis. This will help you with moving forward in the cycling process. You can also watch your fish, as they become more stressed as the water gets worse. The fish in the tank will be releasing ammonia and that is what you want.

Step Four: Feed the Fish

Feed the fish according to the species. You want them to be healthy but you also want to leave them a little hungry since hungry fish tend to expend more ammonia since their stomachs are smaller. You want to make sure that you do not overfeed the fish and also make sure that there is no excess food floating in the tank. Any food the fish doesn't eat will only pollute your tank, which means you will have to start from the beginning.

Step Five: Change the Water Slightly

During the first few days, your fish may be surviving fine. By day three, the bacteria in the tank will be established but it will be at very low levels. What this means is that the ammonia will be really high but the bacteria is starting to do its job. As the bacterium eats the ammonia, it begins to change it into nitrates, which will help to balance your water levels.

By day 5, you may see some of the less hardy fish die. When you see this, you want to change some of the water to help alleviate the levels of ammonia. To do this, remove only 20% of the water from the tank. You can remove less but do not remove more.

Replace the water that you took with fresh water. Make sure you use water that is free of chlorine since this will affect your water quality and you will end up having to start from scratch.

You can add clean water to the tank whenever you feel that the fish are getting stressed from the water conditions. Do not do it every day but once a week should be fine. In addition, make sure that you only remove 20% of the water any time you change it.

Usually, you will find that the water levels are dangerous to your hardy fish on Day 5 and Day 14 but it will be different depending on the number of fish that you have in the tank and the size of your tank.

Step Six: Continue to Monitor Levels

The final step is to continue monitoring the levels in your tank. The goal is to create a good level of bacteria in your filtering system. You don't have to add a lot of different things into the tank as the fish are creating the proper levels on their own.

When you look at the timeline of those 30 days, you should see something very similar to this.

- Prior to cycling: Water is aged enough for the fish to be placed in. In areas where you have high chlorine levels in your tap water, you may need to leave it for up to 7 days.

- Day 1: Hardy fish are added to the tank.

- Day 3: A healthy bacterium begins to be established in your aquarium in low levels.

- *Day 5:* High level of ammonia, some of your hardy fish may die. You can change some of the water.

- *Day 8:* First level of bacteria is established, ammonia begins to lower and nitrites rise. Fish are happier and more active.

- *Day 14:* Nitrite levels are high. Fish appear stressed again. Second stage bacteria occur but is still in low supply so it does not affect the nitrite levels. Water can be changed, again, make sure it is only 20%.

- *Day 29:* Second stage bacteria are established and are turning the nitrites into nitrates. The water becomes more habitable for more delicate fish.

After day 29, you should have two types of bacteria in the tank. One type will eat the ammonia produced by fish and turn it into nitrites. The second type will turn the nitrites into nitrates.

Monitor your tank until you get the desirable readings for pH and then add your fish when it has levelled out.

As I said, it is a long process but after you are finished you will have a perfectly balanced tank that is natural and free of a lot of harsh chemicals.

Once your tank is cycled, your tank set up is complete and you are ready to add your puffer fish, which I will go over in the next chapter.

3. Setting up a Brackish Water Tank

If you have read the chapter on puffer fish species, then you should be aware of the fact that there are many different types you can purchase. One type of puffer fish that you can own is brackish water puffer fish.

For those who are not aware, brackish water puffer fish are puffer fish that thrive in the estuaries that lie between a river and ocean. The water is not as salty as ocean water; however, it is also not as salt free as fresh water.

While we often don't think of it as water for a fish tank, brackish water tanks can be a beautiful display that is teeming with amazing fish and other water life. In this section, we will go over everything you need to know about setting up your brackish water tank.

a) Brackish Water Habitats

Before we get into setting up your aquarium, it is important to note that there are several different types of habitats that you can make in your aquarium. Because of this, how you set up your brackish water tank will be slightly different.

With any type of habitat, there is actually a difference in the amount of salt or salinity, in the water. The amount of salinity is affected by the size of the river or stream emptying into the ocean, the tides in the area and the temperature of the area. Temperature can affect the evaporation rate of the water and this can affect the salinity as well. Most areas that have brackish water have a specific gravity, which is the level of salinity in the water, that varies between 1.0005 and 1.021.

When we look at brackish water habitats, we are actually looking at three different types of habitats, these are:

Brackish Water Habitat One: The River

The first habitat that we are going to look at is known as a river habitat. This is a habitat that occurs when a fast flowing river flows into the ocean. This type of habitat does not usually have a high salinity level but it does have a very high oxygen level.

In addition, brackish river habitats usually have dense plant life on the banks of the river and there should be open spaces in the middle of the river where you have a stronger current.

River habitat aquariums can be more difficult to make since you need to understand the flow of the river. It usually has a very fast current and this can be difficult to recreate in your aquarium.

When you are setting up a river habitat, make sure that you have an aquarium that is no smaller than 30 gallons. There are some aquarists who have made a brackish river habitat with 10 gallon; however, I do not recommend it simply because the smaller tank makes it a bit harder.

Take into consideration the natural habitat that you find in a brackish river. What this means is that you should have rocks and stones as substrates. You should also have a high density of plants, either live or silk, on the sides of the tank. You should also bring the plants up the sides of the tank so the plants cover the top of the water as well. The middle of the tank should be open to give a similar appearance to the river.

To create the much-needed current, use a power head that is designed for your aquarium size. Another piece of equipment that you will need for this type of habitat is an air stone and air pump. Because brackish river habitats are fast flowing, there is usually a very high level of oxygen in the water; this is why an air stone and air pump are a must.

In addition to this equipment, you should keep your salinity at the lower scale. Usually, salinity should be no more than 1.005 to 1.010. PH levels should be the opposite and should be kept fairly high at 7.6 to 8.5. Finally, the temperature of a brackish river aquarium should be at between 78 to 84°F.

One of the biggest benefits of the brackish river habitat is that it can have a high number of fish since there should be an abundance of plant life as well as a high level of oxygen in the water.

Brackish Water Habitat Two: The Estuary

Another type of habitat that you can make is an estuary. This usually occurs when a large river empties out into the ocean. The mouth of the river is large enough for there to be a constant water flow throughout the year and this allows for a permanent brackish habitat.

Generally, the estuary habitat has a higher level of salinity with a specific gravity being in the higher levels than other types of brackish water habitats.

With aquariums that you set up as estuary there are actually a lot of different ways that you can set it up. Remember that this is the mouth of a river and it can have any type of terrain that you would put in a freshwater tank. The best decoration for an estuary set up is rocks of varying sizes and also driftwood.

You should try to keep the size of the estuary aquarium no smaller than 55 gallons. Any smaller and you won't get the best experience from your estuary. Another factor that you should consider with an estuary is to have the temperature between 78 to 84°F. This will shift slightly depending on the fish you are adding but the general rule is to have it at that temperature.

PH balance should also be considered and you will need it at 7.6 to 8.5. Salinity or the Specific Gravity (SG) should change depending on the age of the fish you are putting in your tank. If you are starting off with juveniles, keep the SG at 1.010 to 1.015. If you are starting off with adult fish, set it to 1.20 to 1.025. One thing that is very important is that you increase your salinity as your fish grow until you have the right SG levels for adult fish.

Brackish Water Habitat Three: The Mangrove Swamp

The final type of habitat that you can create for your brackish aquarium is a Mangrove swamp. These can be found in both rivers and estuaries and really, there is a lot that you can do with this type of aquarium set up.

Before you do set up your mangrove swamp aquarium, it is important to be aware of the fact that mangrove swamps usually have a low water flow. In addition, you should be aware of the types of mangroves that can be purchased to make your tank interesting. Mangroves come in several varieties but the most common are black, white and red. They are usually very slow growing trees and while they can reach incredible sizes, you can purchase small trees for your tank without having to worry too much.

Mangrove roots tend to spread out through the tank and there are a variety of roots that come from the tree. Larger roots keep the tree supported in the substrate while smaller roots pull oxygen and nutrients from the water. The roots provide a wonderful place for the fish to hide.

One thing that is very interesting with a mangrove swamp set up is that the mangrove tree is a natural filter. Usually, if you make a mangrove swamp as your tank habitat, then you will not need a filter for the tank.

With the mangrove trees, you should also have a variety of floating plants and driftwood in the tank. The substrate should be rocks.

With regards to the size of your tank, you should have at least a 30-gallon tank. In addition, you should make sure that you have a long tank as opposed to a tall tank. This will give you a more natural habitat for fish that call mangrove swamps home.

As with other tanks, you should have an air pump in the aquarium to make sure that you get enough oxygen in the water for both your fish and your mangrove trees.

Salinity of a mangrove swamp habitat should be 1.010-1.015 and the pH level should be 7.8 to 8.5. Temperature should be 78 to 84°F.

b) Equipment

Equipment for a brackish water aquarium is very similar to the equipment that you need for a freshwater aquarium. There are some differences but again, it depends on the type of habitat that you are creating. If you haven't read it already, take the time to read up on the different habitats that your tank can have.

- Filter: Having a good filter is very important for your fish. There are many different filters out there, but I recommend that you use an Aquaclear or a Marineland filter. They are usually very high quality and they don't break down as quickly as other filters. I also recommend that you purchase a filter that hangs on the back of the tank.

With filters, I strongly recommend that you purchase the right filter for your tanks size. A 50-gallon tank should not have a filter for a 20-gallon tank. In addition, make sure that you use two filters in your tank. The reason for this is twofold. Firstly, your tank will be cleaner. Secondly, you will always have a backup filter running if one filter fails.

- Heater: As you know, puffer fish live in tropical climates. This means that they do require warm water to survive properly. Again, temperature will vary depending on the species of puffer fish that you are putting in the tank. With heaters, I recommend Marineland heaters. They are usually very durable and are perfect for getting the temperature right.

As with filters, I recommend that you use two heaters. The main difference is that you should use smaller heaters instead of one designed for your tank size. For instance, if you have a 100-gallon tank, choose two 50-gallon heaters. Make sure you set them up on either side of the tank to help heat the water thoroughly. The nice thing with having two heaters is that you will find the water stays a more even temperature and if a heater dies, you will have the backup running.

Lastly, it is very important that you choose a heater that can be used in both saltwater aquariums and freshwater aquariums.

- Thermometer: As with all tanks that have to be heated, always make sure that you have a thermometer in your tank to determine the temperature in the water. Make sure that you check it frequently and make sure that the temperature stays in the ideal range. If there is a rise or drop in temperature, it could lead to shock, disease and even death for your puffer fish.

- Hydrometer: A hydrometer is a device that measures the salinity of your water. This is very important for any brackish water tank since you want to make sure that your salinity is always at the proper levels.

- Lid: There are different types of lids and aquarium hoods that you can purchase for your tank but it is important to have one. Some, if not all, species of puffer fish can jump out of the water and it is not uncommon for them to do so. The lid will keep your puffer fish from getting out.

Another benefit of a lid of some kind is that it will keep contaminants out of your tank. Air fresheners, dust, and other outside contaminants can land in the water. Even minute traces of some contaminants can destroy the ecosystem in your tank and make your fish sick.

The only time when you won't be using a lid is with a mangrove swamp since you will have your mangrove trees coming out of the tank itself.

- Substrate: There are many different types of substrate, which is the sand, gravel or rocks that line the bottom of an aquarium, which you can purchase. Really, it is up to the effect that you are going for.

With brackish water habitats, the substrates are usually sandy, silty or muddy. It also has rocks or a combination of all of the substrates.

- Tank Vacuum: There are many different types of tank vacuums that you can use and it is really something that is a preference. I prefer to use a tank python but you can purchase higher quality tank vacuums.

- Aquarium Gloves: Finally, make sure that you purchase a good pair of aquarium gloves. This will enable you to place your hands into the aquarium without the worry of contamination from your skin. In addition, aquarium gloves allow you to handle the fish in your aquarium safely.

c) Decorations

As you know, I have gone over the various items that you should have to decorate your tank according to the habitat that you are creating.

You can use a range of natural and manmade decorations and really, there is nothing holding you back. The only thing that you should remember is that anything that goes into your tank should be clean to ensure that you do not place disease into your tank inadvertently.

d) Chemicals

Although you can treat a brackish water tank in much the same way as you do a freshwater tank, there are a few things that you should have for your brackish water aquarium. These are:

- *Marine Salt:* Marine salt is used for your fish. I recommend that you use Instant Ocean, as this allows for better results when you are increasing the salinity.

- *Water Test Kit:* Make sure that you have a good water test kit that will also test the salinity of your tank. Do not go with just a freshwater or a marine kit but try to find one that works for both. If you can't purchase one of each then use the test kits for testing your water levels.

e) Getting your Tank Ready

Now that you know the various items that you have to have for your fish tank, it is time to start getting it ready. As I have already mentioned, it is very important to wash everything that you are placing in your aquarium. This will help prevent contamination from outside contaminants.

Once you have everything washed, it is time to start setting up your tank. This is not something that I can really guide you through. Read the instructions on any equipment that you have and install it as directed.

Next, do a dry run of how you would like your tank set up. I place the items where I want them and then add the substrate. If an item should be buried slightly under the substrate, then I do this, if not, I pick up the items, pour the substrate under the item and then place it on top.

If you are putting in plants, it is best to wait until you have the water in the tank as some plants need the water to keep from flattening; this is often the case with live plants.

Once you have everything set up, you can begin pouring in the water. The best way to do this is to place a flat dish in the centre of your aquarium and pour the water into the dish so it runs off of the dish. You can also run a hose into the tank and have the water slide down the glass of the aquarium. You do not want a steady stream of water going into the substrate as this will cause the substrate to float in the tank and the water may become cloudy.

When you have the tank filled, you can begin to run your filters and also run your heaters. You want the water to sit for 1 to 2 days to remove all the chlorine without having to use a dechlorinating chemical.

After the one or two days, check the temperature in the tank until you get it to the right temperature. When it is at the right temperature, you can begin to cycle your tank, which is how you get the ph levels to the right stage.

With a brackish water aquarium, I recommend that you cycle the water as you would do with a freshwater aquarium. Read the section on cycling your fish tank.

Once the cycling is done, you can begin to add your marine salt to the tank. To do this, remove your cycling fish. Allow the tank to settle for 24 to 48 hours.

After it has settled, begin adding salt to the tank. You will need to add one tablespoon of salt for every gallon of water. Check your specific gravity reading and add the salt that is required.

One thing that is important is to always remove 50% of the water whenever you need to play with salt levels when you have fish in the tank. By doing this, you will avoid using too much salt.

When your tank is ready, leave it empty for a few more days before checking levels to make sure that you did not affect the levels at all.

Although it may seem like a difficult task, setting up a brackish water tank is actually very easy and outside of playing with salt levels, there really isn't a lot of extra that you need to do.

4. Setting up a Saltwater Tank

The final tank that we are going to look at setting up in this book is a marine tank or a saltwater tank. Although many people think of saltwater tanks as being extremely difficult to set up and maintain, they are actually quite easy. In fact, if you were to ask me which aquarium is the easiest, I would say a saltwater tank.

Before you begin setting up your saltwater tank, there are a few things that you should know. These are:

1. Pay attention to where you place your aquarium.

While you may want to show off your aquarium to the world, the worst thing you can do is to place it in direct sunlight. What this means is that entrance halls with bright sunlight, windows or anywhere where the fish tank will get 4 or more hours of direct sunlight are not appropriate places to put a tank.

The reason for this is because sunlight encourages algae growth and you will end up with a lot of problems in your tank.

2. Go big or go home.

No, you do not need a large aquarium, however, if you are new to saltwater aquariums, it is better to go with a large aquarium. Believe it or not, large tanks are more forgiving than smaller ones.

3. Choose a secure and cool location.

Finally, make sure that the location that you choose for your aquarium is cool and does not have a lot of heat or direct heat blowing on it. In addition, choose a spot where the tank can be level and that it is supported. The last thing that you want is for the tank to fall or shift in any way.

With saltwater tanks, I recommend that you choose a glass tank, as this will give you the best viewing opportunity. In addition, glass has fewer toxins in it so the water will be much easier to care for.

a) Equipment

Equipment for a saltwater aquarium is very similar to the equipment that you need for a freshwater or brackish water aquarium.

- *Filter:* Having a good filter is very important for your fish. There are many different filters out there, but I recommend that you use an Aquaclear or a Marineland filter. They are usually of very high quality and they don't break down as quickly as other filters. I also recommend that you purchase a filter that hangs on the back of the tank.

With filters, I strongly recommend that you purchase the right filter for your tanks size. A 50-gallon tank should not have a filter for a 20-gallon tank. In addition, make sure that you use two filters in your tank. The reason for this is twofold. Firstly, your tank will be cleaner. Secondly, you will always have a backup filter running if one filter fails. Lastly, make sure that it is a filter designed for saltwater tanks as the salt can ruin a filter.

- *Heater:* As you know, puffer fish live in tropical climates. This means that they do require warm water to survive properly.

Again, temperature will vary depending on the species of puffer fish that you are putting in the tank. With heaters, I recommend Marineland heaters. They are usually very durable and are perfect for getting the temperature right.

As with filters, I recommend that you use two heaters. The main difference is that you should use smaller heaters instead of one designed for your tank size. For instance, if you have a 100-gallon tank, choose two 50-gallon heaters. Make sure you set them up on either side of the tank to help heat the water thoroughly. The nice thing with having two heaters is that you will find the water stays a more even temperature and if a heater dies, you will have the backup running.

Lastly, it is very important that you choose a heater that can be used in saltwater aquariums.

- *Thermometer:* As with all tanks that have to be heated, always make sure that you have a thermometer in your tank to determine the temperature of the water. Make sure that you check it frequently and make sure that the temperature stays in the ideal range. If there is a rise or drop in temperature, it could lead to shock, disease and even death for your puffer fish.

- *Hydrometer:* A hydrometer is a device that measures the salinity of your water. This is very important for any saltwater tank since you want to make sure that your salinity is always at the proper levels.

- *Lid:* There are different types of lids and aquarium hoods that you can purchase for your tank but it is important to have one. Some, if not all, species of puffer fish can jump out of the water and it is not uncommon for them to do so. The lid will keep your puffer fish from getting out.

Another benefit of a lid of some kind is that it will keep contaminants out of your tank. Air fresheners, dust, and other outside contaminants can land in the water. Even minute traces of some contaminants can destroy the ecosystem in your tank and make your fish sick.

- Substrate: There are many different types of substrate, which is the sand, gravel or rocks that line the bottom of an aquarium, which you can purchase. Really, it is up to the effect that you are going for.

With saltwater tanks, you can actually avoid a lot of substrate or simply go with basic sand.

-Power Head: A power head is a piece of equipment that goes into your tank to help simulate tidal currents. It is not necessary for all tanks but it is important to check your species of puffer fish to find out if they need an artificial current.

- Air pump: Another item that you will want to have in your aquarium is an air pump to help add oxygen. Again, this is a piece of equipment that is not always necessary and it is actually only necessary if you use a power head.

- Tank Vacuum: There are many different types of tank vacuums that you can use and it is really something that is a preference. I prefer to use a tank python but you can purchase higher quality tank vacuums.

- Aquarium Gloves: Finally, make sure that you purchase a good pair of aquarium gloves. This will enable you to place your hands into the aquarium without the worry of contamination from your skin. In addition, aquarium gloves allow you to handle the fish in your aquarium safely.

b) Decorations

Decorations for saltwater aquariums can range from manmade decorations to living coral and living rocks. If you have any intention of placing a puffer fish into your tank, then I strongly recommend that you do not use any coral or living rocks.

Remember puffer fish eat shellfish in their diet and coral are another favourite meal for them. They will quickly destroy any live coral or rock in the tank. If you plan on aquascaping, which is decorating a marine tank, then plan on using artificial rocks and coral that are designed for saltwater aquariums.

c) Chemicals

Although you can treat a saltwater tank in much the same way as you do a freshwater tank, there are a few things that you should have for your saltwater aquarium. These are:

- *Marine Salt:* Marine salt is used for your fish. I recommend that you use Natural Ocean, as this allows for better results when you are increasing the salinity.

- *Water Test Kit:* Make sure that you have a good water test kit that will also test salinity in your tank. Make sure your test kit is designed for saltwater tanks.

- *Calcium:* Calcium is another important chemical that you need for a saltwater tank if you have any living rock or coral in the tank. If you don't, you can avoid using this chemical.

d) Getting your Tank Ready

Now that you know the various items that you have to have for your fish tank, it is time to start getting it ready. As I have already mentioned, it is very important to wash everything that you are placing in your aquarium. This will help prevent contamination from outside contaminants.

Once you have everything washed, it is time to start setting up your tank. This is not something that I can really guide you through. Read the instructions on any equipment that you have and install it as directed.

Next, do a dry run of how you would like your tank set up. I place the items where I want them and then add the substrate. If an item should be buried slightly under the substrate, then I do this, if not, I pick up the items, pour the substrate under the item and then place it on top.

If you are putting in plants, it is best to wait until you have the water in the tank as some plants need the water to keep from flattening; this is often the case with live plants.

Once you have everything set up, you can begin pouring water in. The best way to do this is to place a flat dish in the centre of your aquarium and pour the water into the dish so it runs off the dish. You can also run a hose into the tank and have the water slide down the glass of the aquarium. You do not want a steady stream of water going into the substrate as this will cause the substrate to float in the tank and the water may become cloudy.

When you have the tank filled, you can begin to run your filters and also run your heaters. You want the water to sit for 1 to 2 days to remove all the chlorine without having to use a dechlorinating chemical.

After the one or two days, check the temperature of the tank until you get it to the right temperature. When it is at the right temperature, you can begin to add salt to your tank. You will cycle your tank later on but for right now, you simply want to get the salt to the right level.

With adding salt, I recommend that you follow the packaging and add it as directed. If you are worried about getting the right salt levels, you can purchase premixed salt water. It is a bit more expensive but it does make setting up a saltwater tank easier.

One thing that is important is to always remove 50% of the water whenever you need to play with salt levels when you have fish in the tank. By doing this, you will avoid using too much salt.

After your salt levels are ready, you can begin to cycle your water as you would do with a freshwater tank. Follow the directions on cycling your tank.

Once it is cycled, allow it to settle for a day or two before you begin adding fish to your aquarium.

Chapter 7. The Puffer Fish Community

Now that you have your tank set up, it is time to really focus on the community that your puffer fish will be entering into. In this chapter, I will go over some of the partners that you can put in with your puffer fish without too many problems.

In addition, I will go over how to add your puffer fish to an already established community so that you do not put the puffer fish and the other fish at risk.

1. Pairing Puffer Fish with Other Fish

As I have gone over several times through this book, puffer fish are predators and for that reason they are not always recommended for community aquariums. Before you add more than one type of fish to your aquarium, it is important to read up on your specific species. Some puffer fish are more aggressive than others and there are a few species that should never be placed in a community aquarium.

Generally, if you are creating a community for your puffer fish, I recommend choosing larger fish. The main reason for this is because puffer fish will often eat any fish that is smaller than they are. In addition, some puffer fish may be fin nippers so they may eat the fins off of your larger fish. A good rule of thumb that I follow is to have faster, larger fish in the tank to prevent a lot of problems.

a) Brackish Water Partners

When it comes to brackish water partners, it is important to look at them separately from freshwater partners. The reason for this is because there are some slight differences in the types of fish that you can keep in a brackish water aquarium. Fish that make good companions for brackish water puffer fish are:

83

Barbs:

Barbs are one of the best fish to keep in a community tank that has a puffer fish. They tend to be fast swimmers, which makes it harder for the puffer fish to attack them. In addition, barbs are usually more aggressive so this will usually create a prey reaction from the puffer fish. When the barb swims near the puffer fish, they will often hide from them.

With barbs, there are many different kinds, however, for a brackish water aquarium, I recommend tiger barbs as they can usually handle the salinity. In addition, make sure that you purchase at least three barbs for your tank since they are a species that swim in schools.

Bumblebee Gobies:

Bumblebee Gobies are another fish that do very well with puffer fish and it is not because of their size. In fact, many bumblebee Gobies are smaller than puffer fish species but for some unknown reason, puffer fish avoid eating them.

Bumblebee Gobies have a beautiful black and yellow banded pattern on their bodies. They do not have scales and they have a suction-like fin that allows them to attach to the sides of the tanks. They are not overly aggressive but they are extremely fast fish and have no problem out swimming a puffer.

Cichlids:

It is important to note that not all cichlids can do well with puffer fish so it is important to really be careful when you are partnering a cichlid with a puffer fish. This fish can actually be very beautiful and they come in a variety of colours and species.

They can be aggressive fish and many will bite the puffer fish, which will lead to the puffer fish leaving the cichlid alone. Cichlids do very well in brackish water conditions.

Mollies:

Another fish that does very well with puffer fish are mollies. Again, they tend to be faster swimmers than puffer fish and they have no problem staying away from them. In addition, they can be aggressive and will often attack any fish that tries to nip them. Like the cichlids, this will often be enough of a deterrent for a puffer fish.

There are many varieties of mollies that you can choose from but avoid any that are ornate since their ornate tails and fins can be a target for a puffer fish. Mollies do very well in both brackish water and freshwater aquariums.

Plecos:

Plecos are a type of catfish that seem to do very well with puffer fish. It is actually very surprising since they are not a fast swimming fish and they are not overly aggressive. Still, many puffer fish species will leave a pleco alone and the pleco itself will aid in keeping the tank clean.

One important thing to remember with plecos is size. These fish can get to be quite large so it is important to check the species before you purchase it. In addition, you should only have one or two per tank but no more.

Scats:

The final fish that you can put in a brackish water puffer fish community is a scat. These are a tank cleaning fish and they will usually eat any waste that the puffer fish puts into the tank. I strongly recommend these fish as they will help keep your tank sparkling clean and they are actually quite pretty.

Like the pleco, scats do well with puffer fish and are usually not bothered by the puffer fish. Again, there is no known reason why this is but it can be very easy to keep two or three of these in a puffer fish tank. They do the same job as a pleco; however, they don't grow as large as the pleco, which makes them a great companion in a smaller tank.

And there are the best fish for a brackish water community. Although some aquarists tell you not to have any other fish in your tank with a puffer, there are a few species that can do very well.

b) Freshwater Partners

When it comes to freshwater companions for your freshwater puffer fish, there isn't a lot to choose from. Again, freshwater puffer fish can be very aggressive and some species should never be in a tank with other fish.

Some companions that you can have for a freshwater aquarium are:

Barbs:

Barbs are one of the best fish to keep in a community tank that has a puffer fish. They tend to be fast swimmers, which makes it harder for the puffer fish to attack them. In addition, barbs are usually more aggressive so this will usually create a prey reaction from the puffer fish. When the barb swims near the puffer fish, they will often hide from them.

Mollies:

Another fish that do very well with puffer fish are mollies. Again, they tend to be faster swimmers than puffer fish and they have no problem staying away from them. In addition, they can be aggressive and will often attack any fish that tries to nip them. Like the cichlids, this will often be enough of a deterrent for a puffer fish.

There are many varieties of mollies that you can choose from but avoid any that are ornate since their ornate tails and fins can be a target for a puffer fish. Mollies do very well in both brackish water and freshwater aquariums.

Plecos:

Plecos are a type of catfish that seem to do very well with puffer fish. It is actually very surprising since they are not a fast swimming fish and they are not overly aggressive. Still, many puffer fish species will leave a pleco alone and the pleco itself will aid in keeping the tank clean.

One important thing to remember with plecos is size. These fish can get to be quite large so it is important to check the species before you purchase it. In addition, you should only have one or two per tank but no more.

Again, the type of fish that you can add to a freshwater puffer fish aquarium are limited but you can find some truly beautiful specimens in these fish species.

c) Marine Partners

Puffer fish being kept in a marine community tank has been met with mixed results. Some aquarists have mentioned that their puffer fish are aggressive to all other fish so they are not able to house any, while other aquarists have had very few problems.

In general, if you are trying to house a marine puffer fish with other tank mates, it is important to make sure that the fish that you place with your saltwater puffer fish are larger and swim faster.

Some fish that do well with marine puffer fish are:

Wrass:

Wrass fish are an excellent fish to partner with puffer fish since they tend to be aggressive fish that will bite back if the puffer fish bites. There are a wide variety of wrass fish to choose from and most of them are quite small. In fact, there are over 500 species of wrass so the options are limitless.

Tang:

Another great fish for a marine aquarium are tangs. These fish are brightly coloured and very beautiful. They are fast swimmers and will usually out swim an aggressive puffer fish. There are a wide variety of tangs that you can purchase and I strongly recommend getting one for your puffer fish tank.

And those are the two fish that I would recommend for a marine puffer fish aquarium. Some aquarists have had success with angels and other types of marine fish so the rule of thumb is to make sure that you choose carefully and always have a second tank ready in case the community fails.

d) Puffer Fish as Tank Mates

Although we could look at this topic when we look at the partners for specific tank types, I would prefer to address it separately. Many people new to aquariums are unsure whether or not puffer fish can do well with other puffer fish as tank mates.

While I wish there was a clear answer to that question, the truth of the matter is that it really depends on the species and the tank set up. A large tank with ample space can accommodate several puffer fish; however, a smaller tank will cause territorial problems.

In addition, some puffer fish do very well with other puffer fish because they are less aggressive. When you are deciding whether to pair puffer fish together, you should consider these things.

1. What is the species?

Always make sure that you check the species before you mix the puffer fish together. While it may not seem like a problem, some puffer fish species are highly aggressive and will attack other puffer fish. These battles aren't minor and it can often be to the death.

2. Can they survive in the same conditions?

Make sure that when you choose two different puffer fish that they can survive in the same conditions. For instance, you could never pair a freshwater puffer fish with a marine puffer fish.

Usually, this is not an issue. However, when you have a brackish water aquarium, there are some puffer fish that need a low salinity level and others that need a high salinity level. These two puffer fish should never be housed together.

3. Is there enough room?

I have already touched on this but make sure that there is enough room for both puffer fish. Remember that they are usually very territorial and they will attack each other when they are resource guarding. If you provide enough room, along with enough food, you should be fine housing more than one puffer fish in a tank.

4. Are they male and female?

As you already know, determining the sex of a puffer fish can be difficult so this is not always something that you can see. With a few species, such as the Dwarf puffer fish, you can identify the male and female. Generally, males and females can do well in a tank together. However, housing two puffer fish of the same sex can be very dangerous, especially if you add a third puffer fish that is the opposite sex.

For anyone that is just starting out in the world of aquariums, I would recommend only having one puffer fish in the tank at once. After that, research the species thoroughly before you add more than one and make sure that you have a second tank ready just in case your puffer fish begin to fight.

2. Adding a Puffer Fish to an Established Community

Now that you know what type of community a puffer fish can go into, it is time to look at adding your puffer fish to that aquarium. When you are introducing a puffer fish to an aquarium, there are a few tips that you should remember.

1. Add the puffer fish to an established community.

One of the biggest mistakes that an aquarist can make is to create a new aquarium and then add the puffer fish first. The reason for this is that a puffer fish will quickly become territorial over his tank and will attack any new fish you bring in.

Instead, have it established and allow the puffer fish to find his place in the community. This will help to avoid creating a bully and I have seen more success doing this method of introduction than by adding other fish after the puffer fish has claimed the tank.

2. Be prepared to separate.

Another mistake that you can make with puffer fish is to not have another tank ready and waiting on the off chance that the puffer fish can't settle into the tank without fighting.

Be prepared to separate and don't be too upset if you get a puffer fish that needs to be kept on his own. It isn't the end of the world for the puffer and you can always enjoy two different types of aquariums.

3. Always check water levels at the store.

Another important part of adding a puffer fish to a new or established aquarium is to ensure that the water levels match. Check the store to find out what their water levels are and then match them in your quarantine tank.

As your fish is going through quarantine, adjust the levels slowly until it matches up with the levels in your main tank. This will give your puffer fish the chance to become accustomed to the levels and will help prevent a lot of problems from occurring when you transfer the puffer fish.

4. Feed the puffer fish when you transfer.

I always recommend that you feed the puffer fish when you transfer them to help focus the puffer fish on eating what you give him and not on eating the other fish. In addition, if you feed either right before transferring or as soon as he calms down, the puffer fish will spend time exploring his new surroundings and less time hunting down some food.

When you do feed him after a transfer, make sure that it is several hours after he has been moved and that the meal is small.

5. Float your puffer fish.

Finally, when you are adding puffer fish to a new tank, always make sure that you float the container that the puffer fish is in. Do this for several hours until the temperature of the water in the container is the same as the temperature of the water in the aquarium. This will help prevent the puffer fish from going into shock at the sudden temperature changes.

Whenever you get a new fish, regardless of whether it is a puffer fish or not, you should acclimate it before you transfer it to a new tank. This helps the fish make the transfer without experiencing any shock when it happens.

There are actually two different ways to acclimate a fish and these are floating and drip acclimation and in the next section we will go over both.

a) Floating a Fish

Floating a fish is one of the most common methods used for acclimating a fish to a new aquarium. It is fairly simple to do and there isn't a lot that you need to do to be successful in floating a fish. To float a fish, follow these steps:

1. Remove the lid from your aquarium. Make sure that you turn off any lights in your aquarium as this can cause stress for your new fish.

2. Place the tied bag or the specimen container into the aquarium. Do not open the container or bag but allow it to float in the aquarium for about 15 minutes. The main reason why you do not open it at this point is that it keeps a high level of oxygen in the water for your fish.

3. Once it has floated for 15 minutes, cut the bag or open the container. Roll the bag inwards and down so there is about a 1-inch pocket of air in the bag to keep it floating. If you are using a

specimen container, it should attach to the aquarium to keep from sinking. Allow it to float for another 15 minutes.

3. Once it has floated for an additional 15 minutes, take a ½ cup of the aquarium water and pour it into the bag or container. Leave it for five minutes.

4. After 5 minutes, add another ½ cup of water to the bag or container. Repeat this process every 5 minutes until the bag is full of water.

5. When it is full, lift out the bag and throw away half of the water from the container. Do not pour it back into your tank but throw it out completely. Also, be careful not to pour out your fish.

6. Place it back in the aquarium, again, floating it for 5 minutes. After the 5 minutes, add another ½ cup of water to the bag from the aquarium.

7. Repeat the process, adding another ½ cup every 5 minutes until the bag is full.

8. When the bag is full, take a net and carefully remove the fish from the container. Release it into the tank.

9. Remove the bag filled with water and discard the water. To avoid disease, never pour the shipping water into your aquarium.

b) Drip Acclimatizing a Fish

Drip acclimation is another way to acclimate your fish to their new aquarium. This is a more involved process but I find that it works best for many types of fish. It is an absolute must when you are acclimatizing a sensitive fish such as a puffer fish.

1. Remove the lid from your aquarium. Make sure that you turn off any lights in your aquarium as this can cause stress for your new fish.

2. Place the tied bag or the specimen container into the aquarium. Do not open the container or bag but allow it to float in the aquarium for about 15 minutes. The main reason why you do not open it at this point is that it keeps a high level of oxygen in the water for your fish.

3. After it has floated in the aquarium water, remove it from the aquarium. Cut open the bag and pour the water and fish into a clean 3 to 5 gallon bucket. Tip the bucket if necessary to keep the fish completely submerged in water. Brace it so the fish is not exposed to air.

4. Using an airline tube, siphon water from the main aquarium through the line. You will need to use an airline control valve to make sure that you do not add too much water into your bucket at one time. You can purchase an acclimation kit to do this properly. To siphon the water, you will need to suck on the tube until the water is flowing and then adjust the airline control valve until you have a rate of 2 to 4 drips per second.

5. Place the airline tube into the bucket and allow it to slowly fill. When you double the amount of water in the container, discard half of the water. Be careful not to dump the fish out when you discard the other water.

6. Return the drip line to the bucket. Allow the water to double again.

7. When it has been doubled, take a net and carefully remove the fish from the container. Release it into the tank.

8. Discard the water. To avoid disease, never pour the shipping water into your aquarium.

c) Quarantining your Puffer Fish

The last thing that I want to go over with regards to adding your puffer fish to the community is quarantining. As you know, I have mentioned quarantining several times throughout this book and it is a very important step in adding a fish to your tank.

If you are not sure as to why it is important, the first thing to look at is that many pet shops have aquariums that are over populated. What this means is that there is a greater chance of health problems due to poor water quality. In addition, many of these pet shops do carry disease in their tanks and the last thing you want is to bring that home to your already established community.

Lastly, many, if not all, puffer fish that are purchased in a pet store are from the wild. This means that they can have a wide range of parasites and other illnesses that affect fish in the wild.

To properly quarantine your fish before you add them to your tank, follow these steps:

1. Set up a small aquarium.

Read the chapter on setting up your aquarium and make a small aquarium according to the recommendations. Remember that you should have the exact same water quality levels in the quarantine tank as your main aquarium. If the pet shop has them at a different water quality level, make sure you adjust it slightly, as I mentioned in the last section.

2. Bring your fish home.

Once your quarantine tank is set up, it is time to bring home your new puffer fish. Although it may be tempting to bring more than one puffer fish home at a time, avoid doing this. Remember, puffer fish can fight and a small quarantine tank is more likely to cause one.

When you bring your puffer fish home, make sure that you acclimate him to the tank before you put him into it. Do not just pour his water out into the aquarium or you will shock the fish and that can result in death.

3. Give your fish a chance to recover.

Moving to a new tank is always stressful so make sure that you give him a day to relax and recover from the move. You don't have to start giving him treatments or doing anything else with the puffer fish. You simply want him to get back to his normal activities and be completely shock free when you move on to the next step. The only thing that I would recommend is a light feeding several hours after he is in the tank but other than that, leave him alone.

4. Medicate your puffer fish.

After the fish has had a chance to recover from the move, it is time to put some medicine into the water. This should be done on day two of your new fish being in the tank. Follow the instructions on the bottle and use Prazipro, which helps cure fish of worms and other parasites. It is very gentle and can work well on puffer fish.

4. Change the water.

After you have treated the fish, wait until day seven before you do anything else, other than feed the puffer fish. On day seven, do a water change of the tank. It is very important that you remove 25 to 50% of the water and refill it with old water or water that has no chlorine in it. Make sure that you bring all the levels back up to what the tank was originally.

5. Medicate with Cupramine.

Once you have the levels back up to what they were before, medicate the water with Cupramine. This is a medication that helps with a number of diseases including ich and velvet. It is very important to monitor the copper levels in the water after you add this medication, as too much copper is deadly to the fish. Always start out with a small dosage and then slowly raise it according to the package.

6. Administer Prazipro for the second time.

Although some aquarists do not recommend mixing any medication with Cupramine, Prazipro is one medication that you can mix safely and I strongly recommend it. After you have given the fish a day to recover from the cupramine medication, add in another dose of prazipro. This will help get rid of any worms or other parasites that the first dosage missed.

7. Quarantine for two weeks.

Once the medication has been given, it is time to allow your fish to rest in quarantine. Check him on a daily basis to make sure there are no signs of infection or other problems. If you see an infection, treat with Marcyn-two, which is a broad spectrum antibiotic.

8. Release into your main tank.

At the end of the two weeks, or after 21 days from the first day it went into the tank, you can move the fish into your main aquarium if there are no other signs of disease or parasites.

To do this, place the fish into a specimen container and then drip acclimate the fish to the main tank.

When the acclimation is done, transfer just the fish to the new tank. Do not add the water from the quarantine tank to the main aquarium or you could risk infecting your main tank.

It is a long process but aquarists that quarantine every new fish they bring home are much more likely to have a long and happy life with their fish.

Chapter 8. Caring for your Puffer Fish

When it comes to caring for your puffer fish, there really isn't a lot of extra care that you need to do in addition to the care we have gone over in this book. For the most part, puffer fish are fairly hardy fish and they just need a tank that has proper water quality. After that, it is simply a matter of watching the puffer fish's health and feeding him.

That being said, there are a few things that you should do for the everyday care of your puffer fish and I will go over all of these things in this chapter.

1. Transporting Your Puffer Fish

The very first thing that I want to mention is transporting your puffer fish. Many people make a lot of mistakes when they are transporting puffer fish and even pet stores make these mistakes.

The first thing that you should know is that puffer fish have very strong jaws and teeth. While this may not seem like something that you need to worry about during transporting, it is. Puffer fish have been known to bite through bags when they are being transported.

To help prevent this, I recommend purchasing a small igloo cooler and having the pet store place the puffer fish directly into the cooler with the water from the aquarium. Make sure that you use multiple coolers if you are purchasing more than one puffer fish.

Another factor that you should take into consideration when you are transporting is the duration of the journey. If you are going a long distance, you should purchase a battery-powered aerator. These can actually be purchased at fishing shops. Attach the aerator to your cooler so that the fish receives the proper amount of oxygen throughout the journey.

If you are simply transporting your puffer fish between tanks, it is very important not to use a net. Most puffer fish species will become startled when a net closes over them and they will puff up. You want to avoid this, as you don't want to stress the fish out too much.

Instead, use a specimen container to scoop the puffer fish up without the use of a net. This will make transporting much easier on them and will ensure that he won't become stressed.

2. Dental Care

For many puffer fish, there is not a strong need for dental care if they are being fed a proper diet. If the diet is not done properly, then you will be tasked with the job of dental care on your fish.

Puffer fish dental care is very serious and it should be done properly. If you are new to puffer fish, I strongly recommend that you get a vet or someone with experience in caring for puffer fish to trim the teeth of the puffer fish.

To trim the teeth, follow these steps:

1. Remove the fish from the main tank and place him in a specimen bucket with water from the tank.

2. Add in a small amount of MS-222, which can be purchased from your vet. Make sure you follow the directions given to you by the vet or you could risk killing your puffer fish. MS-222 is a common medication to euthanize aquariums so be very careful with it.

3. Next, take clove oil, which can be purchased from most drugstores, and add 4 drops per litre of water. Again be very

careful when you are using this because clove oil is another medication that will kill your fish.

4. Once you have given the fish the two medications, it is time to work quickly. Have a helper wet his hands down and then hold the puffer fish. I recommend wearing aquarium gloves for this. The reason why you give the two medications is because the puffer fish is sedated enough to be able to handle it without it puffing up, which is the last thing you want.

5. As soon as the fish is secured, take a pair of cuticle cutters and trim back the teeth slightly. You do not have to do much if you are caring for the teeth properly.

6. Once they are cut back, place the puffer fish into a second bucket that is filled with unmedicated aquarium water. Allow him to recover in the second bucket, make sure you monitor him the entire time. When he has recovered, you can return him back to the aquarium.

One thing that I stress when you are administering dental care for your puffer fish is to work quickly. Usually, a puffer fish will be calm enough to handle within 30 seconds of the clove oil being administered. After that, you should only take a few minutes to trim the teeth. If you take too long, your puffer fish could become ill from the medications that you are using.

Although dental care may be necessary, if you are properly taking care of your puffer fish, you shouldn't have to worry about trimming the teeth back.

3. Puffing

Another factor that you should take into consideration is puffing. This is very common with puffer fish as it is a natural way for them to protect themselves when they feel threatened or scared.

Puffing is when the puffer fish will expand its body and expose the spines on its body to prevent a predator from eating it. While many puffer fish owners will encourage this reaction, it is very important that you do not.

Remember that puffer fish only puff up when they are scared or threatened. This means that the puffer fish are feeling extreme stress and this stress can lead to the puffer fish becoming sick or even dying.

It is important to reduce stressors in the puffer fish's environment and to avoid doing anything that will make the puffer fish puff.

4. Aquarium Care

The final thing that we are going to look at is maintaining the aquarium. This is very important when it comes to puffer fish care and is one of the most time consuming aspects of owning a puffer fish.

A properly maintained aquarium will ensure that your puffer fish remains healthy. In addition, it will ensure that your puffer fish is happy and that the life of all of your fish is extended.

When it comes to aquarium care and maintenance, there are three rules that you should follow. These are:

1. Do not have too many fish.

Follow the guidelines for each fish when it comes to the number of gallons they need. Never exceed the number of fish in the tank for the number of gallons needed. The more fish you have, the harder your tank will be to maintain. In addition, the more fish you have, the greater the chance that the fish will become sick.

2. Do scheduled water changes.

Although many people feel that you can simply add the water and leave it, this is not the case. Do a partial water change several times per month. Take out 20% of the water from the tank and discard it. Once you discard it, fill the tank with dechlorinated water. This will help keep ammonia, nitrates and nitrites at appropriate levels. In addition, it will help keep your filter working properly.

3. Do not overfeed.

Lastly, make sure that you do not overfeed your fish. If you do, you will find that it is difficult to keep the aquarium clean and the water quality will be very poor. This will lead to a higher chance of disease in your aquarium and your fish may begin dying because of it.

If you follow these three rules with your aquarium, you will find that you will only need to deal with the aquarium care once a week.

Every week, you should carry out the following steps.

1. Take an aquarium safe cloth and wipe the front and sides of the glass on the outside.

2. Take a second aquarium safe cloth and wipe the inside of the glass to wipe away any residue that has formed on the glass in the water.

3. At this point, take your gravel vacuum and vacuum the gravel. You want to remove as much dirt and debris from the gravel as this is usually where the fish leave food. The food will decay and lead to higher levels of ammonia in the tank.

4. While you are vacuuming, take out about 10 to 20% of the water. This can be done every ten days but I find that it is much easier to do it weekly. Make sure you replace the water with de-chlorinated water.

And that is really all you need to do on a weekly basis. Every two to eight weeks, you will need to clean and change the filter. In addition, you should remove the carbon in the filter when you are doing the filter cleaning. Other than that, if you have followed the three rules, your aquarium will stay clean and you won't have to do much else.

Chapter 9. Your Puffer Fish's Diet

Before we look at the various foods that you should be feeding your puffer fish, it is important to remember that every puffer fish species has different needs. Because of this, you should research your individual puffer fish to find out what he eats.

While we do cover diet in this chapter of the book, the main focus is on the general diet that is commonly seen in most puffer fish species. Always check with your seller on the specific needs of the puffer fish that you are purchasing. Once you do that, you won't have too many problems regarding feeding your puffer fish.

1. Tips for Feeding Puffer Fish

A few things that I want to point out about a puffer fish's diet before we look at the actual food your puffer fish will be eating are:

1. Puffer Fish Prefer Live Food

Although you will find puffer fish food in many pet stores, dry flakes are not going to keep your puffer fish happy and healthy. In fact, most puffer fish will ignore flakes and other dry or dead food. What they prefer is live food. Remember, puffer fish are predators so they do enjoy hunting.

While there are many benefits to providing live food for your puffer fish, there are also some negatives. These can be having parts of dead fish in your tank, which can lead to health problems. In addition, many feeder fish can carry diseases of their own, which can be dangerous to your fish.

Although there are risks with live food, I strongly recommend it as providing your puffer fish with prey can help curb, and at time eliminate, some aggressive behaviour in your fish.

2. All Live Food should be Quarantined

This goes hand in hand with feeding live food but it is something that needs to be addressed separately. As I have mentioned, live food can carry a number of diseases and parasites that can be transferred to your puffer fish.

To help prevent that, keep your live food in quarantine for several days before you allow the puffer fish to eat them. I recommend that you do a week to several weeks of quarantine and to have several tanks set up so that you are not reinfecting your feeder fish when you add new feeders to the tank.

3. Offer a Little Variety to your Puffer Fish

Another important tip with regards to feeding is to offer your puffer fish a variety of foods. While you can stick to one or two different types of food, puffer fish do enjoy a number of different fish to eat. In addition, puffer fish do require some hard-shelled food in their diet as this will help keep their teeth ground down.

In addition to care, giving a puffer fish a variety of food will help prevent many problems in your tank. For instance, if a puffer fish is not given hard-shelled food, he may begin attacking the decorations in your tank to work his teeth. If you have coral, you can expect your coral to be destroyed very quickly as the puffer fish will choose the coral for his food.

4. Feed on a Daily Basis

Puffer fish do much better when they are getting a daily diet as opposed to every few days. The rule of thumb is to feed your puffer fish once per day, usually in the morning. If you feed more than once per day, you can end up overfeeding the puffer fish, which leads to many problems, including constipation. If you feed less than once per day, your puffer fish could end up starving.

5. Use a Feeding Stick

One of the most entertaining aspects of a puffer fish is that they are often called the "puppy dog" of the aquarium. They do bond with their owners and will often come up and beg for food at the top of aquarium. It is actually this behaviour that causes many puffer fish to be overfed but if you exercise restraint, you can begin to teach your puffer fish to take food from hand.

Remember that feeding by hand is a figure of speech and you should never feed the puffer fish directly from an unprotected hand. It may not seem like it, but those teeth are sharp and can hurt.

Instead, take a feeding stick and attach a piece of food to it. Move the stick so the food looks like it is alive and swimming. When the puffer fish attacks the food, release it from the feeding stick and then offer him a bit more. The amount of food your puffer fish will eat in one feeding session will depend on the age and size of your puffer fish.

Remember that feeding your puffer fish does not have to be too complicated and if you get in the habit of feeding on a daily basis, you won't have to do too much.

2. Basic Diet for your Puffer Fish

As I have mentioned, most puffer fish will have some diet differences depending on the species of puffer fish they are. Having said that, the majority of puffer fish will share the same diet and you can find both freshwater and saltwater equivalents to the food that I will go over in this section.

Although I will be going over the food that you can feed your puffer fish, it is important to note that I will not be going over quantity. This differs depending on the size of your puffer fish and also on what you are feeding him.

A good tip for feeding is to watch the stomach of your puffer fish. If the stomach looks lumpy, then the puffer fish has eaten enough. If it has no bulk to it at all, then the puffer fish needs more food. Finally, if the puffer fish's stomach is hard and engorged, then the puffer fish has overeaten.

Never use the puffer fish's behaviour to gauge whether it has eaten enough. A puffer fish is often a food hog and they will beg and continue to eat even after they are full.

Now that you know many of the tips and how to gauge if your puffer fish is full, it is time to look at the food that you can feed him.

1. Krill:

Krill is a small, shrimp like animal that can be purchased for marine aquariums and it is a great food for puffer fish, especially when they are young. You can buy krill from many pet stores and you can also purchase it frozen to feed to freshwater or brackish water puffer fish. If you are using frozen krill, make sure you feed from a feeding stick. In addition, be prepared for your puffer fish to turn his nose up at it. Some wild puffer fish will not eat anything frozen as it seems unappetizing.

2. Snails

I love snails for a number of reasons. One, they are usually very inexpensive. Two, you can purchase snails for your tank and they will help keep your tank clean whilst providing a food source for your puffer fish. And three, they will breed very quickly so you can keep a breeding tank for the snails and have a constant supply of food for your puffer fish.

Snails can be found in several varieties and they are a hard-shelled food that will help wear down the puffer fish's teeth.

3. Bloodworms

Often, people don't think of bloodworms as a food for puffer fish, but they are actually a very good food. Bloodworms are the larval stage for flies. They are high in protein and are often a staple food for puffer fish. Like krill, you can purchase bloodworms live, or you can purchase them frozen or dried. Again, puffer fish that are taken from the wild may not eat the frozen or dried bloodworms.

4. Red Glassworms:

These are the same as bloodworms and are simply the larvae of mosquito. Puffer fish usually enjoy this food and they are high in protein.

5. Shrimp:

There are several different types of shrimp that you can choose from and it really depends on the size of your puffer fish. Most puffer fish will eat ghost shrimp, whereas larger species can eat full sized shrimp. You can also purchase frozen shrimp and cut them up to feed them to smaller puffer fish. One thing to remember is that some frozen shrimp is washed in chlorinated water and this can cause some stomach problems for your puffer fish.

Another important thing to stress about shrimp is that this should not be your fish's primary diet. Puffer fish love shrimp and it can be very easy to offer just shrimp to your fish, however, they need a wide variety of foods to get the proper nutrients.

6. Molluscs

Clams, oysters and other shelled molluscs are excellent for puffer fish since they offer them high protein meat along with the hard shells that will wear the teeth down. With molluscs, it is important to make sure that they have not been washed in chlorinated water like shrimp have.

7. Feeder Fish

Small feeder fish can make a great food for puffer fish but again it is not something that should be the primary food source for your puffer fish. Feeding feeder fish once or twice a week, along with all of the other foods, will help provide a well balanced diet for your puffer fish.

8. Crustaceans

Finally, you can feed your puffer fish crustaceans such as red-clawed crabs and crayfish. Again, this offers them both a hard shell and high protein meat.

Remember that whatever you choose for your puffer fish, you want to make sure that you quarantine the live food to ensure that your puffer fish will not suffer any ill effects.

Chapter 10. Your Puffer Fish's Health

When it comes to puffer fish health, caring for them is not too difficult. They usually have very little health problems and puffer fish tend to be fairly hardy if they are in the right type of aquarium. If you have not read the chapter on setting up your aquarium, I strongly recommend that you do so.

In this chapter, I will go over everything that you need to know regarding puffer fish health and how to care for your puffer fish when he is sick.

1. Keeping Your Puffer Fish Healthy

Although this entire book works towards keeping your puffer fish healthy, there are a number of things that you should do specifically for your puffer fish health. If you are thinking in terms of rules that apply to caring for a puffer fish, you should always remember three rules. These are:

1. Avoid Stress

Puffer fish, along with many other types of fish, can suffer greatly if they are stressed in any way. But many people new to aquariums are never sure what stressing a fish entails so it is important to look at it in these terms:

- *Water Levels:* As we all know, poor water quality can be detrimental to the health and happiness of your fish. PH levels that fluctuate can create a lot of stress for your fish. This is even truer for fish without scales, such as the puffer fish. They can be very sensitive to spikes and drops in pH and will suffer poor health because of it.

- *Water Temperature:* This falls in the same category as water levels. Remember that puffer fish are tropical fish. If you have constant fluctuations in the water, the fish is going to become stressed. Once the puffer fish is stressed, its immune system will weaken and it will be susceptible to illnesses.

- *Tank Set Up:* How you set up your aquarium can also affect your puffer fish and cause stress. Most puffer fish require places to feel sheltered, if there are no hiding places in the aquarium, your puffer fish is going to feel stressed. Make sure that there are broad-leafed plants and caves for your puffer fish.

- *Current:* As you may know, some tanks need a current running through it but it is very important to make sure that your current is not too strong.

- *Tank Companions:* The final thing that you should consider when you are trying to keep your puffer fish healthy is the tank companions that he has. Some puffer fish do well with companions whilst others suffer from severe aggression and should be on their own. Although we don't often think of it, aggression can create stress for the puffer fish.

2. Feed it a Proper Diet

We have gone over this in length on our chapter regarding feeding your puffer fish. This is very important and is something that you should be doing for your puffer fish. Although many people are not aware of it, puffer fish eat a wide range of foods. In addition, puffer fish require hard-shelled food to help keep their teeth filed down.

In addition to a proper diet, it is important that you do not overfeed them. Puffer fish will often gorge themselves on food if it is presented to them. Too much food can lead to health problems, including constipation, so it is important to avoid this. The general rule of thumb is to only feed your puffer fish once a day. If you are not sure if he is eating enough, look at his stomach. A lumpy stomach is a well-fed puffer while a large, round and hard stomach is one that has been overfed.

3. Do a Daily Health Check

One of the best ways to keep your puffer fish healthy is to really pay attention to it. Check the fish on a daily basis and make sure that there are no signs of disease or illnesses. Often, if you catch an illness early, you can correct the problem without too much damage to your fish.

When you are doing a health test, make sure that you look the fish over completely. Check for damage from other fish such as bite marks, nibbled fins or open wounds. Also check to make sure that there is normal gill movement and that the fish has normal activity levels.

Another thing to look for is any parasites or external signs of disease. You should also watch your fish and make sure that it is swimming properly and that there is nothing unusual about the way it swims.

If you follow these three rules with your puffer fish, you should be able to keep him healthy and happy for a long time.

2. Signs of Disease

Before we go over the diseases that can affect your puffer fish, it is important to understand the signs of disease. There are actually many different signs and they will differ depending on the disease.

As I have mentioned, do a daily health check on your fish and look for the following signs:

1. No appetite: If you find that your puffer fish has lost his appetite, or doesn't seem to be eating much, you should monitor him for other symptoms. Many times, that loss of appetite is the first sign of an illness.

2. Darkening of the belly: This is only seen on fish with lighter bellies or with white bellies. Usually, when a puffer fish starts feeling ill, the belly will begin to darken slightly. It will go from white to a light grey. If the problem is left without treatment, the grey will continue to darken until the puffer fish's belly is nearly black.

3. A dark grey line: Another symptom that affects colouring is the appearance of a line. This line will start on either side of the mouth and will extend down the body to the tail. It is usually found between the dorsal and belly markings on the fish.

4. Lethargy: A fish that seems to be swimming very slowly and does not have the energy levels that it normally has is almost certainly sick.

5. Floating near the surface: While all fish will spend time at the surface of the tank from time to time, if your fish is hovering at the surface constantly, something is wrong.

6. Shifts in dorsal colouring: Again, colouring can be very important in determining if your puffer fish is ill and the dorsal colouring can help to identify ill health. If it suddenly darkens or begins to fade, something is wrong. It is important to remember that some puffer fish will change colour according to their mood so make sure you do not have that type of puffer fish before you worry about shifts in your puffer fish's colour.

7. Loss of mobility: Another sign is if your fish has a sudden loss of mobility. Although puffer fish are clumsy fish, if you see it crashing into decorations or into the sides of the tank, check him over for more symptoms. They do not usually have these problems.

8. *Rapid respiration*: Finally, if the puffer fish looks as though he is gasping for air at any time, he may be suffering from an illness or he may be stressed.

In addition to these symptoms, make sure that you know the symptoms of common diseases that can affect your puffer fish. By knowing the symptoms, you can treat your puffer fish quickly and see him on the road to recovery before the disease does any lasting damage.

3. Common Diseases

In this section, we will go over all of the common puffer fish diseases that can occur in your tank. It is important to be aware of these things and to treat them immediately when you see them.

a) Black Spots

This disease is usually not seen in tanks unless you are bringing wild fish into your tank, hence the importance of a quarantine tank. This is actually a parasite that thrives in cold water. It is actually a larva for an adult parasite that lives inside birds. When the birds relieve themselves over water, the eggs land in the water and hatch. The larvae then attack the fish.

The symptoms of black spots are a large, cyst like spot that has a black colouring. It can also appear as a yellowish cyst on puffer fish that have little pigment.

The treatment for black spots is formalin. It is important to read the directions on the bottle and to follow them. However, you should only administer half of the recommended dose. Remember, since puffer fish do not have scales, they are more sensitive to this treatment than other fish are.

b) Vibriosis

Vibriosis is a very dangerous disease that occurs when there is an injury on the fish. The disease itself enters the fish through the injury and causes further damage to the immune system and body. Usually, this disease is more common in marine or saltwater tanks than in any other tank, however, there have been strains found in freshwater tanks.

Symptoms of Vibriosis are skin lesions, skin haemorrhaging, popeye and distended bellies. If it is not treated quickly, usually with antibiotics such as furazolidone, it can be fatal to the fish.

c) Popeye

Popeye is a disease that is commonly caused by bacteria found in the water. The bacteria get into the system of the puffer fish and cause an infection that leads to pressure building up behind or inside the eyes. This makes them "pop". It is important to note that some illnesses can cause a symptom of popeye so you need to be careful when you are diagnosing this disease.

As I have mentioned, a symptom of popeye is a swelling in and around the eye. The eyes begin to protrude from the eye socket and have an appearance like they are about to pop out. In addition to the swelling, there is often cloudiness in the eye.

Treatment for popeye is usually antibiotics such as maracyn-two.

d) Ammonia Poisoning

Ammonia poisoning is a very common problem that many aquarists have faced at least once in their life. It is caused by the fish that you place in the tank. Generally, what happens is that the fish produce too much ammonia and the bacteria in the tank are unable to eat it fast enough.

Ammonia poisoning can be prevented by adding fish to the tank gradually and also by having a properly cycled tank. If you do both of these, along with keeping your tank clean, you shouldn't have any problems with ammonia.

Symptoms of ammonia poisoning can be as minor as your puffer fish looking as though it is gasping for air. As the poisoning gets worse, the puffer fish may begin to darken in colour. Lastly, the gills will begin turning red and may even begin bleeding.

Treatment for ammonia poisoning is in correcting the ammonia levels in your tank. There is nothing that you can do for the individual fish and hopefully, with proper cleaning of the tank, your puffer fish's health will correct itself.

For treatment, remove 20% of the water and replace it with old water that is free from chlorine. In addition, clean the tank and remove any uneaten food, rotting plants or anything else that will produce a lot of ammonia.

When the tank is clean, add in a small amount of an ammonia remover such as Amquel to remove the ammonia from the tank.

For your puffer fish specifically, add in a small amount of stresscoat, which is a slime restoring solution.

e) Cottonmouth

Cottonmouth is a type of bacteria that can be found in a puffer fish's mouth. It is usually found in the cheeks of the puffer fish; however, it can also be seen in other parts of the mouth.

When the bacterium gets into the puffer fish, it creates a tuft of cotton like material in the mouth. As the cotton like material grows, the fish begins to appear sluggish. In addition, the puffer fish will stop eating. Another sign that you may see is swollen lips on the puffer fish.

Treatment of cottonmouth is usually done with antibiotics such as maracyn-two. In addition, it is important to clean the carbon in your filter.

One of the most important steps that you should take with this tank is to quarantine it. Do not use any nets, aquarium gloves or anything else that you used in the tank on any of your other tanks. Cottonmouth is highly contagious and it has even been known to spread on the hands of an aquarist when he does not wash his hands between tanks.

f) Bends

Also known as gas bubbles, puffer fish can suffer from bends, which is when there is a super saturation of nitrogen in your tank. The main cause of this is due to the nitrogen levels being high in your tank. When they are high, the fish breathes it in and an embolism is caused. Gas bubbles obstruct the blood vessels.

Puffer fish that are suffering from bends are usually very lethargic. Generally, one of the best indicators of whether you have a high nitrogen level in your tank is if there are bubbles on the sides of the tank and also on the fish itself.

Treatment of bends is done by treating the water and removing the nitrogen that is in the water. It is very important to make sure that you place the puffer fish in a different tank until you get the water cycled and the super saturation of gas worked out.

g) Ick

Ick, also known as fish lice, is a disease caused by a parasite that attacks the host and burrows into the body of the fish. Since puffer fish do not have scales, they are usually more susceptible to ick and it can be difficult to cure.

Symptoms of Ick are laboured breathing as well as a fish that looks like it is itchy. Your puffer fish may scratch against the various decorations in the tank. One of the most definable symptoms is visible, raised spots on your puffer fish that look like grains of salt.

These grains of salt are the encapsulated parasite and when they burst they can actually lead to secondary infections that can be deadly to the fish.

Ick is highly contagious and it needs to be treated quickly when it is seen. To treat ick, you must follow these steps:

1. Quarantine the aquarium as soon as you see ick. This means that you should not share equipment such as nets and vacuums with other tanks that you have.

2. Vacuum the tank. Take the time to vacuum the gravel in your tank and you should do this several times while you are treating ick.

3. Add a small amount of salt to the water. On a daily basis, you should add about 3 teaspoons per gallon of marine salt to your tank. This can be done with freshwater tanks as well.

4. Change the water every day that you are carrying out treatment. Make sure that you are replacing about 25% of the water every day while you are doing the treatment for ick. Usually, I recommend that you do it the day after you give

medication. Usually, this is every 3 to 4 days for about 12 to 14 days.

5. Treat the tank. The recommended chemical that you should treat your tank with is Maracide. Follow the directions on the bottle to be sure that you use it properly.

6. Raise the temperature of your tank to the maximum temperature that your fish can endure. This will help speed up the lifecycle of the parasite, which will enable you to get rid of it faster.

When you are treating ick, it is very important to watch your puffer fish and make sure that he is not distressed at any time. In addition, watch for any signs of a secondary infection.

h) Myxobacteriosis

This disease is actually not that common and is something that many aquarists will not come across. With regards to information on this disease, there is actually not a lot. What we do know is that it is an infection that leads to black patches on the fish. This can occur on the body or fins.

It is believed to be caused by poor water quality in the tank; however, it is not clear if it is brought on by high ammonia levels or by high nitrite levels.

The only treatment for myxobacteriosis is Phenocide. This is made by Aquatronics and has been designed to combat this disease specifically.

i) Black Chin

Black chin is another disease that is not always that common in puffer fish and it is one that not much is known about it. It is believed to be caused by nitrate poisoning since it has commonly occurred in tanks where the nitrate levels are greater than 25ppm.

The symptoms of black chin usually manifest themselves as small grey-black patches that appear on the lower jaw of the fish, hence its name. In addition, the fish may develop a stress line, which is a line that will start on either side of the mouth and will extend down the body to the tail. It is usually found between the dorsal and belly markings on the fish. A tank symptom of black chin is usually a high level of algae.

Treatment of black chin should be done by cleaning the tank frequently. In addition, you should change the water levels of the tank by changing out 20% of the water every 3 to 4 days until the levels are back in the normal range.

j) Nitrite Poisoning

Nitrite poisoning is a disease that occurs when there is a high level of nitrites in the tank. It is a disease that attacks the haemoglobin, which is the red pigment in your puffer fish's blood. This transformation takes a blood cell that transfers oxygen through the body and turns it into a methaemoglobin, which cannot transfer blood.

The symptoms of nitrite poisoning are gasping and increased gill movement. The fish may also begin being stressed in the tank and will be very agitated. If this is not treated properly and quickly, the puffer fish can die from this problem.

Treatment for nitrite poisoning is in correcting the nitrite levels in your tank. Make sure that you remove your fish to a properly cycled tank with low nitrite and ammonia levels.

While it is in the other tank, remove 20% of the water and replace it with old water that is free of chlorine. In addition, clean the tank and remove any uneaten food, rotting plants or anything else that will produce a lot of ammonia, which also indicates a high level of nitrites.

k) Nitrate Poisoning

Nitrate poisoning is very similar to other forms of poisoning that your puffer fish can experience such as nitrite and ammonia poisoning. It is caused by a high level of nitrates in the tank and this is usually caused by overcrowding, overfeeding and even irregular water changes.

In addition to these causes caused by poor maintenance, high nitrate levels can occur if you live in an area with high nitrate levels in the drinking water.

Symptoms of nitrate poisoning are loss of appetite, poor colouration or colour shifts in the skin, lethargy, increased respiration and the fish may be itchy. Nitrate poisoning can be fatal to the fish it can often be difficult to treat. The poisoning is often too advanced once you begin seeing symptoms.

Treatment for nitrite poisoning is in correcting the nitrite levels in your tank. Make sure that you remove your fish to a properly cycled tank with low nitrite and ammonia levels.

While it is in the other tank, remove 20% of the water and replace it with old water that is free of chlorine. In addition, clean the tank and find the source for the high nitrate levels so you can remove them.

l) Dropsy

Dropsy is a disease caused by bacteria called Pseudomonas punctata. This bacterium invades the puffer fish's body and attacks the internal organs of the fish. The fish may experience deformities because of this disease and it can result in death if it is not treated quickly.

Symptoms of dropsy are a swelling in the body cavity of your puffer fish and ulcers or lesions on the skin. You may also see a loss of equilibrium when your puffer fish is swimming.

Dropsy is treated with an antibiotic such as Maracyn-two along with some partial tank changes of the water. In addition, it is imperative that you remove any dead fish from the tank immediately as it can often be spread when the puffer fish eat the dead fish.

m) Velvet

Velvet is another disease that is caused by an organism known as Oodinium pillularis. It is a parasite that attaches to the fish's skin and gills and grows until it begins attacking the host body that it has adhered too.

It usually manifests itself as tiny specks of yellow spots that often look like dust on your puffer fish. In addition, your puffer fish may begin to have laboured breathing and may also have a loss of appetite.

Like many diseases, the best way to treat velvet is to use maracyn-two as recommended on the bottle. In addition, you should use a half dose of maracide in the water to kill the parasite itself.

n) Carbon Dioxide Poisoning

Carbon dioxide poisoning occurs when there is a high level of carbon dioxide in the water. When the fish breathes it in, the oxygen carrying pigment in red blood cells stops transporting oxygen through the fish's body. This leads to several problems including death.

Carbon dioxide poisoning usually occurs as a result of overcrowding in a tank. It is also commonly seen in new fish that have had to travel great distances to get to the store or to your aquarium.

Symptoms include loss of appetite and also increased breathing. As I mentioned, carbon dioxide poisoning can result in death.

The best treatment for carbon dioxide poisoning is an influx of oxygen. Place the fish in an oxygen rich tank until its health has been restored. If the fish has collapsed, hold the fish in your hands in the water and move it back and forth slowly. This will help with the flow of oxygen over the fish's gills.

Although placing the fish in an oxygen rich tank is beneficial while the fish is in the tank, it is very important to check the oxygen levels in its primary tank. If they are low, correct it by placing an air pump in the tank.

o) Fin Rot

Also known as tail rot, this disease is caused by bacterial infections. This is commonly the result of poor water conditions; however, it can also be the result of a wound that becomes infected.

Fin rot is often noticed when a ragged fin begins to occur on the fish. The fins and tail on the puffer fish may look like they have split or may even look clumpy, almost as though it has melted. The fin and tail will continue to erode until the bacterium begins to attack the actual body of the fish.

Treatment of fin rot is usually done with antibiotics such as maracyn-two. In addition, it is important to clean the carbon in your filter.

One of the most important steps that you should take with this tank is to quarantine it. Do not use any nets, aquarium gloves or anything else that you used in the tank on any of your other tanks. Fin rot is highly contagious and it has even been known to spread on the hands of an aquarist when he does not wash his hands between tanks.

p) Chlorine Poisoning

Chlorine poisoning is caused when there is a high level of chlorine in the tank water. It is actually one of the easiest illnesses to avoid since it simply requires you to avoid using tap water that hasn't been treated with dechlorinator or aged until the chlorine is gone.

Symptoms of chlorine poisoning are trembling, shifts in colouration and a stress line, which is a line that will start on either side of the mouth and will extend down the body to the tail. It is usually found between the dorsal and belly markings on the fish.

The fish may also try leaping from the water and will also dart around the tank. There may also be increased breathing. A fish can die from chlorine poisoning if it is not treated properly and quickly.

Treatment of chlorine poisoning is to remove the fish from the offending tank and place it in a tank free of chlorine. If you do not have a secondary tank to do this, use a dechlorinator in the tank. This can be risky since some dechlorinators can be harmful to fish so it is important to monitor your fish while you are treating the chlorine.

q) Fungal Infections

Fungal infections can occur due to a number of different funguses that grow in tanks. They usually occur as a secondary infection after the puffer fish has a weakened immune system. They are caused by a variety of factors; however, temperature often plays a key role in the growth of fungus in your tank.

Symptoms of a fungal infection are a cotton like growth on the fish's body or thin threads of skin growing off of the fish. Many times the fungus begins on the body but it can move on to the eyes, tail and fins. It can also cause deformities to occur in the fish.

Treatment should be done with maroxy or methylene blue and by adding small amounts of salt to the tank. On a daily basis, you should add about 3 teaspoons per gallon of marine salt to your tank. This can be done with freshwater tanks as well.

r) Hypoxia

Hypoxia is a condition that can often result in the death of your fish. It occurs when there is a lack of oxygen being transported through your fish's body. This leads to the puffer fish's tissue dying and can be very serious. There are many reasons as to why hypoxia occurs but it is often due to other illnesses or infections such as carbon dioxide poisoning.

Symptoms of hypoxia are increased breathing, shifts in coloration, lack of movement in the eyes and swimming at the surface. During the later stages of hypoxia, the fish may have difficulty moving from the bottom of the tank. In addition, a stress line will appear, which is a line that will start on either side of the mouth and will extend down the body to the tail. It is usually found between the dorsal and belly markings on the fish.

Treatment of hypoxia should consist of treating the underlying condition that is causing the hypoxia. In addition, you should add extra oxygen to the water and help the fish get oxygen into its gills by moving it back and forth in the water.

And those are the most common health concerns that you will face with your puffer fish. Remember that having good water quality will help prevent many of these diseases, as will quarantining any fish that you purchase before adding them to the tank.

Chapter 11. Breeding your Puffer Fish

When it comes to breeding, there really isn't a lot of information that I can give you. For the most part, puffer fish breeding has been unsuccessful. In fact, many species of puffer fish have never bred in captivity.

Before you decide on trying to breed your own puffer fish, it is important to note that there are a few challenges that you are going to be faced with.

One: The sex of a Puffer Fish is hard to Determine

The first thing that you should be aware of is it is very difficult to determine the sex of a puffer fish. Males and females of the majority of species look similar, if not identical. This means that successfully choosing a male and female for your tank is all about luck.

Two: Puffer Fish Need Ideal Conditions

It is clear that puffer fish need ideal conditions for breeding. This means that they need to have the right water levels along with the right habitat. What is not clear is what those perfect conditions are.

Three: Puffer Fish Young are Difficult to Care for

Although breeding has occurred occasionally and eggs have been produced, the successful raising of young is not easy. Young are extremely difficult to care for and they tend to be very picky when it comes to eating.

Although it would be ideal for puffer fish to be raised in aquariums, the majority of puffer fish are caught from the wild. Another place that puffer fish are bought from are farms. Again, farmed fish are not in tanks but are usually kept in netted off areas in their natural habitats. This is why farmed puffer fish will breed but puffer fish in aquariums will not.

1. Encouraging Breeding

Although I have mentioned that breeding is not something that usually occurs in captivity, puffer fish have been known to breed. If you manage to get both a male and female puffer fish in your tank, there are a few things that you can do to help encourage breeding between the two.

- Keep the water levels at the ideal for the breed. This is very important as this is often when breeding is seen between puffer fish.

- Keep the puffer fish fed. As with most species, breeding usually occurs more frequently when there is an abundance of food. If there is no food for the puffer fish, then the chances of your puffer fish breeding will go down significantly.

- Have a variety of caves. The more caves and other shelters you have in an aquarium, the better chance you will have of your puffer fish breeding. Although puffer fish species vary, many will lay their eggs on plants, or in hollows of natural terrain. Many puffer fish males will guard their eggs from predators.

While it is not a lot, these few steps will help to encourage breeding. Whether they will hatch and grow to full size is strictly up to your care.

2. The Eggs

If you luck out and manage to produce some eggs, you will find that the best thing to do is to sit back and allow the puffer fish to deal with the eggs on their own. If you can, remove any predators from the tank that may prey on the eggs. Generally, the male puffer fish will protect the eggs but it is better to be safe than sorry.

When you see puffer fish eggs, begin to monitor them on a daily basis. Some aquarists will remove the eggs and place them in a new aquarium, however, that can cause damage to the eggs and kill them. I recommend that you leave them in the nesting site until they hatch. Remember, puffer fish are still wild animals and will guard their young in the same in the tank as they would in the wild.

3. The Hatchlings

If you end up being lucky enough to have the eggs hatch, it is very important that you move the larvae, or young fish into a separate tank. You need to do this quickly as young fish are often prey to other fish in your tank.

With the secondary tank, it is important to keep pH levels in the low range and to also keep the salinity low for brackish water puffer fish. The main reason for this is because brackish water puffer fish usually lay their eggs in fresh water and the young live in the rivers before they move down into the estuary.

Although it is not clear what young puffer fish eat, some success has been had with feeding them insect larvae. Small white worms and maggots have been successful but it is unclear if they get full nutrients from this food or not.

The best advice that I can give you is to try a variety of food for your puffer fish hatchlings until you find something that they will eat.

When you have young, you should expect a high percentage of them to die. While it is not completely clear, some fish species will eat each other while they are young. Since puffer fish are predators, you should expect this from your puffer fish young.

As they grow, if you are successful in raising them, slowly raise the pH levels of your hatchling aquarium until it is at the right level for your puffer fish species. In addition, if you have brackish water puffer fish, slowly raise the salinity until you have the proper levels for juveniles.

Once they reach juvenile age, you can decide to either transfer them to your aquarium or to sell them. Remember to also quarantine the young before you transfer. Yes, they may not have any illnesses but it is better to be safe than sorry.

It is important to note that the guidelines that I have given you for raising puffer fish and breeding them is very basic as puffer fish are not successful breeding in captivity. There are only a handful of successful breedings and most of those did not result in a viable adult puffer fish.

Chapter 12. Common Terms

So you are interested in owning a puffer fish. Well, if you want to be a true puffer fish lover and owner, it is important to understand a few of the common puffer fish terms that you will hear the moment you enter the puffer fish raising world. Below is a list of terms and words that you will hear in the puffer fish world.

- Ammonia: A gaseous compound that is found in the decaying plant life of an aquarium and also in the waste of fish.

- Anal Fin: The small fin found on the bottom of the fish right behind the anus of the fish.

- Aquarist: A person who owns and manages a home aquarium.

- Aquarium: a tank or bowl that is made of glass where aquatic animals are kept in water.

- Aquascaping: Decorating a marine tank

- Brackish Water: Water that is a combination of salt water and fresh water, commonly found in the mouth of rivers where they empty into the ocean.

- Carnivore: An animal that eats meat as its primary food source.

- Caudal Fin: The tail fin of the fish.

- Dorsal Fin: A fin or several fins that are found on the back of the fish.

- Gills: The organ found on the sides of the fish that enable the puffer fish to breathe under water.

- *Herbivore:* An animal that primarily eats vegetation and plants as its main food source.

- *Mandible:* Used to describe the lower and upper jaws of a beak.

- *Olfactory Pit:* A small pit or hollow on a fish where the nose should be.

- *Omnivore:* An animal that eats both plants and meat.

- *Pectoral Fin:* Fins that are found on either side of the fish slightly behind the head.

- *Pelvic Fin:* Two fins found on the bottom of the fish near the tail.

- *Salinity:* The amount of salt found in the water of a saltwater or brackish water tank.

- *Specific Gravity:* The term used to measure the amount of salt in the water.

- *Substrate:* The base materials that are placed on the floor of the aquarium.

- *Tetraodontidae:* The Latin name for puffer fish.

- *Truncate:* A tail that has a square look to it or a flat edge at the end of the fin.

- *Undulated:* A wave like movement; usually used in association with describing fin movement.

Photo Credits:

Page 15: © Dreamstime.com 4780342
Page 38: © Dreamstime.com 3998084

CPSIA information can be obtained
at www.ICGtesting.com
Printed in the USA
BVHW041244190319
543078BV00017B/660/P